An Outdoor Family Guide to

ACADIA
NATIONAL PARK

Lisa Gollin Evans

An Outdoor Family Guide to
ACADIA
NATIONAL PARK

Lisa Gollin Evans

THE
MOUNTAINEERS

*To my parents, my family, and especially my wonderful and giving friends,
Julie, Lis, Maureen, Michele, and Patty. From my heart, I thank
you all for being there. It made all the difference.*

Published by
The Mountaineers
1001 SW Klickitat Way, Suite 201
Seattle, WA 98134

First printing 1997, second printing 2000, third printing 2003

Published simultaneously in Great Britain by Cordee, 3a DeMontfort Street, Leicester, England, LE1 7HD

Manufactured in the United States of America

Edited by Kris Fulsaas
All photographs by the author unless otherwise noted
Chapter opening illustrations by Gracie Evans
Cover design by Watson Graphics
Book design by Bridget Culligan
Book layout by Jacqulyn Weber
Typography by The Mountaineers Books

Cover photograph: *Gorham Mountain (Lisa Gollin Evans)*
Frontispiece: *Gracie Evans (Lisa Gollin Evans)*

Library of Congress Cataloging-in-Publication Data
Evans, Lisa Gollin, 1956–
    An outdoor family guide to Acadia National Park / by Lisa Gollin
Evans.
        p.   cm.
    Includes bibliographical references and index.
    ISBN 0-89886-528-X
    1. Outdoor recreation–Maine–Acadia National Park–Guidebooks.
2. Hiking–Maine–Acadia National Park–Guidebooks. 3. Canoes and
canoeing–Maine–Acadia National Park–Guidebooks. 4. Acadia
National Park (Me.)–Guidebooks.   I. Title.
GV191.42.M2E83   1997
917.41'450443–dc21   97-19040
                                                                 CIP

 Printed on recycled paper

Contents

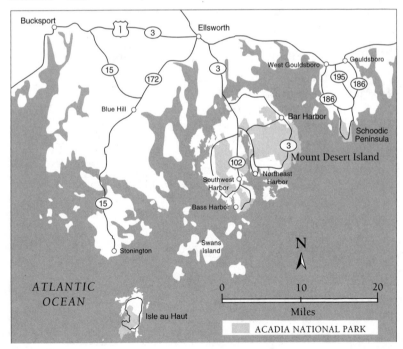

Acknowledgments

Although my name alone appears on the cover, this book was truly a collaborative effort. It could not have been accomplished without the help and support of my family and friends. For this book, as well as for all my previous guides, my husband Frank was often by my side as I hiked, paddled, and cycled through the park from dawn to dusk. His good company and sound advice continue to make all my books the best they can be.

I also thank my daughters, Sarah and Grace, for their enthusiastic participation. Their happy faces are my joy and inspiration on the trail, and keep me coming back for more. Also inspiring is the constant, generous, and loving support of my mother, who always finds a way to help me in these far-flung places. Last, but certainly not least my faithful friend, Julie Strong, and her terrific daughters, Laura and Catherine, once again joined me on my adventures and made my work infinitely easier and more enjoyable.

New to my list of acknowledgments are old friends Joanne Wallenstein and Glenn Fishman and their children, Robert, Julia, and Adrienne, and Elise Blumberg and David Graham and their children, Nora and Aron. Both families I thank for their patience with my endless and painstakingly slow picture taking.

I would also like to thank park ranger Ted Combs of Acadia National Park, who supplied me with a wealth of helpful information and who led so many informative and entertaining walks covering nearly every aspect of the park. Also extremely helpful was Don Beal of Acadia National Park, who supplied me with indispensable information on the Schoodic Peninsula. I would also like to acknowledge the helpful guidance of Jerry Keene, owner of the Cove Farm Inn, the most family-friendly bed-and-breakfast I have ever encountered.

Finally, I would like to express my sincere gratitude to Margaret Foster and Cynthia Newman Bohn at The Mountaineers Books, who were terrifically helpful, patient, and understanding during the writing of this book.

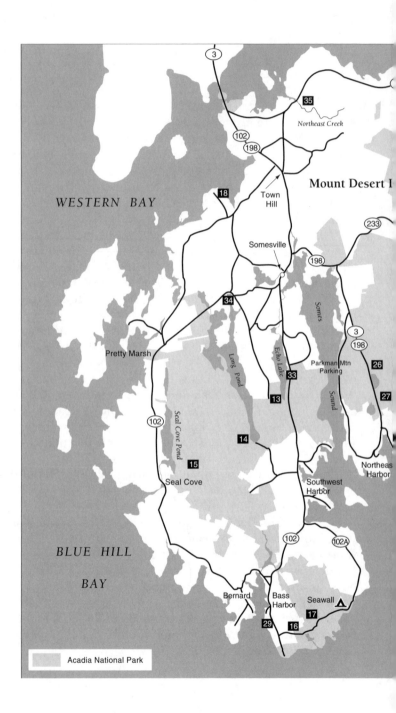

WESTERN BAY

Northeast Creek

Mount Desert I

Town
Hill

Somesville

Somes

Parkman Mtn
Parking

Pretty Marsh

Long Pond

Echo Lake

Sound

Seal Cove Pond

Seal Cove

Southwest
Harbor

Northeas
Harbor

BLUE HILL

BAY

Bernard

Bass
Harbor

Seawall

Acadia National Park

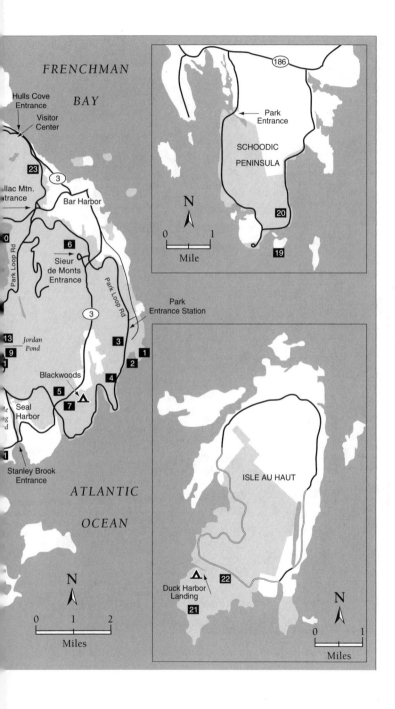

FRENCHMAN

BAY

Hulls Cove
Entrance

Visitor
Center

23

③

llac Mtn.
trance

Bar Harbor

0

Park Loop Rd

6

Sieur
de Monts
Entrance

③

Park Loop Rd

13

*Jordan
Pond*

9

Blackwoods

5

7

Seal
Harbor

Stanley Brook
Entrance

ATLANTIC

OCEAN

N

0   1   2

Miles

186

Park
Entrance

SCHOODIC

PENINSULA

20

N

0   1

Mile

19

Park
Entrance Station

3

1

2

4

ISLE AU HAUT

22

Duck Harbor
Landing

21

N

0   1

Miles

Forest friends (photo: Elise Blumberg)

Introduction

Acadia National Park is full of family adventures, and this book is filled with easy ways to make them happen. Choose from thirty-five exciting hiking, biking, and paddling outings, selected specifically for families. Each outing introduces parents and children to extraordinary features of the park, and each description alerts them to animals, plants, and other natural and historic features that they might otherwise miss. The book also includes detailed information on additional adventures, such as park interpretive programs, camping, whale watching expeditions, sailing, swimming, picnicking, rainy-day activities, and more.

How to Use This Book

Before setting out on any outing, consult this Introduction for tips on hiking, biking, and paddling with children, safety considerations, wilderness ethics, park regulations, and essential equipment. More specific information on Acadia National Park, including its campgrounds, lodging, weather, natural history, and myriad recreational opportunities, follows in Chapter 1. Chapters 2 through 6 provide detailed trip descriptions, organized by type of activity (hiking, biking, or paddling) and geographic region. The outings are classified as very easy, easy, moderate, or strenuous, according to their length, starting elevation, high point, and terrain. For hiking outings, very easy and easy hikes are generally 0.5 mile to 2 miles one way; moderate hikes are 2 to 4 miles; and strenuous hikes are over 4 miles.

In general, this book follows the rating system set forth by Acadia National Park for describing its own trails. "Very easy" indicates a smooth path over level ground, often accessible to wheelchairs with assistance. "Easy" trails indicate uneven but fairly level ground. "Moderate" trails include some steep grades as well as level stretches, and "Strenuous" trails incorporate steep grades and often many steady climbs. To help you quickly choose an outing that fits your needs, appendix A, Trip Finder, concisely lists information such as difficulty, distance, location, and attractions.

Outing descriptions do not provide estimates of hiking, biking, or paddling time. Hikers, bikers, and boaters, especially children, travel at such varied speeds that general approximations would not be reliable. To estimate roughly the time required for a hike, use the average walking rate of 2 miles per hour on level ground for adults carrying packs, plus 1 hour for each 1,000 feet of elevation gain. Rough terrain and hiking children obviously increase the time needed. After a few hikes, you can work out estimates for your own family. Generally, strenuous hikes require a full day; moderate hikes, a half day; and easy hikes, 1 to 3 hours.

At the end of the book are several valuable appendices, including appendix A, Trip Finder. Appendix B, Recommended Reading, contains a bibliography for children and adults of books on nature and the area's natural and regional history. Appendix C, Conservation Organizations, provides information on organizations working to protect Acadia National Park and surrounding areas.

Tips on Hiking, Biking, and Paddling with Children

CHOOSE THE RIGHT OUTING

Pursuing a route that is too difficult for your children is sure to lead to frustration for all. Read outing descriptions carefully to find trips that match your children's abilities. If you are uncertain how far they can walk, bike, or paddle, choose a trip that has intermediate points of interest, so that you can shorten it if necessary. Try also to match your youngsters' interests with a trip's particular attractions, whether they include fishing, rock climbing, swimming, tide pooling, or berry picking.

BRING PLENTY OF SNACKS

Let children snack liberally on their favorite treats while on an outing. They will be working hard, and snacks high in carbohydrates and sugar boost their energy. Also, salty snacks are good for replacing salts lost through perspiration. Good-tasting treats can also be used as a motivating force for reaching the next rest stop. Do not forget to bring plenty of water or juice, particularly in summer, when temperatures are high. Mild dehydration causes crankiness in children, and more severe cases can cause extreme discomfort.

MOTIVATE, MOTIVATE, MOTIVATE!

There are numerous ways to motivate children on an outing. The promise of a picnic or a treat is enough for some. For others, encouraging good-natured competition with siblings or peers does the trick. When a child's motivation wears thin, distraction can be the best solution. Songs, trail activities, games, and stories often invigorate sluggish youngsters. Consult appendix B, Recommended Reading, for books containing trail and nature activities.

LET THE CHILDREN LEAD

Allow children to lead the group when appropriate. When the novelty wears off, assign the lead role to another, rotating the honor among the youngsters. The trail will fly by!

SLOW THE PACE

Let children determine the pace. Progress may be slower, but the trip will be much more enjoyable. Adults also benefit from slowing down: you may cover only half the distance, but you will experience twice as much.

MAINTAIN A POSITIVE ATTITUDE

Praise children for all their achievements on the trail. Positive reinforcement for beginners is essential for building a solid base of good feelings about outdoor adventures. Refrain from criticism if children disappoint you. Scolding will not improve their performance; it will only guarantee unhappiness.

BRING THE RIGHT STUFF

Pack items in your backpack to keep children happy on the trail, especially when hiking. Magnifying glasses, binoculars, cameras, junior field guides, bug-collecting bottles, sketchbooks, or

Friends enjoying the woods

materials for simple projects like bark and stone rubbings provide welcome diversions for youngsters. A child-size walking stick can also provide miles of enjoyment for a young hiker.

RELAX AND ENJOY

When hiking, biking, and paddling with children, the joy is in the process, in the small achievements and discoveries you share along the way. To appreciate this, you must relax. You may miss the thrill of a peak, but the quiet rewards of sharing nature will last a lifetime and will build a strong foundation for your next trip.

Wilderness Ethics

To protect the natural treasures of Acadia National Park, it is essential that visitors follow a simple code of wilderness ethics.

MAKE A POSITIVE IMPACT

The rule of Positive Impact goes beyond the oft-repeated "Take only pictures; leave only footprints." That maxim falls short in today's overcrowded parks. My rule of Positive Impact asks that visitors leave the park a better place. By picking up waste, for example, you enhance the beauty of the trail for the next visitor. Give children a small bag to stuff in their pocket for their own litter and for stray wrappers left by others. Parents should carry litter bags, too.

A second way to create a positive impact is to set a good example by hiking, biking, and paddling joyfully, attentively, and considerately. The model is contagious. Just as a crowd gathers to look at a sight in which others show interest, other hikers will follow your lead if you find a trail interesting, fun, or exhilarating.

DO NOT FEED THE ANIMALS

Do not feed the small mammals and birds that beg for handouts. Feeding is dangerous for you and the animals. Human food harms wildlife in several ways. First, snack food is a poor nutritional substitute for an animal's natural diet. If handouts become a primary source of food, the animal may become malnourished and prey to disease and injury. Second, feeding an animal disrupts its natural foraging instincts. As a result, animals that depend on human feeding may not survive the winter. Third, human feeding unnaturally concentrates animal populations. An unusually large population of birds or squirrels at a picnic area leaves that population vulnerable to epidemic disease.

Feeding wild animals is also dangerous for people. Small mammals may carry rabies, a potentially lethal disease. Rabies aside, the bite of a rodent's sharp incisors is painful. Second, fleas carrying bubonic plague have been found on rodents. Although rare, instances of human contraction of bubonic plague from flea bites have occurred.

LET WILD PLANTS FLOURISH

From May through September, wild gardens grace Acadia National Park. To ensure that all have an opportunity to enjoy the lush array of flowers, ferns, mosses, lichens, and fungi, visitors must refrain from picking even one specimen. Removing plants means removing seeds, thus preventing annuals from reproducing. Also, by removing plants and seeds, you eliminate critical food for the park's wildlife. Lastly, watch your step! While exploring natural areas, stay on designated trails to avoid crushing delicate plants underfoot and disturbing habitat.

STAY ON THE TRAIL

To maintain the integrity, beauty, and safety of trails, do not shortcut. Shortcuts are most tempting where a trail switchbacks down a steep slope. When hikers aim straight down a slope, they damage the vegetation between the switchbacks and cause erosion. If shortcutting occurs frequently, a trail may wash away, leaving a scarred and barren hillside. Also, leaving the trail on a precipitous slope is dangerous and may cause one to fall or lose the trail entirely.

OBSERVE PARK RULES

A few of the most important, and most commonly violated, National Park Service regulations, are the following:
- Carry out all refuse. Leave no waste on trails.
- Do not cut, remove, deface, or disturb any tree, shrub, flower, or other natural object. Carving on trees scars them permanently and can even kill them if the carving girdles the tree.
- Camp only in designated campsites at Seawall, Blackwoods, and Isle au Haut Campgrounds. There is no backcountry camping in the park.

- Use only dead and downed wood for firewood. Never break branches from standing trees, even if they appear dead. The tree may still be living, and breaking a branch may injure it. Build fires only in designated firepits in campgrounds and picnic areas.
- Removal of rocks, plants, fossils, or cultural artifacts from the park is prohibited.
- Edible plants, mushrooms, and berries may only be picked for your daily consumption. *Never* eat any plant that you cannot positively identify. Poisonous plants, including mushrooms, grow in the park!

Enjoying the spring lupine

- Hunting and trapping are prohibited.
- Freshwater fishing requires a Maine fishing permit for those over 11 years of age. Permits are available at most sporting-goods and hardware stores and at town offices in Bar Harbor and surrounding communities. No permit is required for ocean fishing.
- Pets are allowed in most areas of the park, but must be kept on leashes no longer than 6 feet. Pets are not allowed at Sand and Echo Lake Beaches, at Isle au Haut Campground, on ladder trails, or in park buildings.
- The use or possession of firecrackers or fireworks is prohibited.

BIKE RESPONSIBLY

Acadia National Park is a bicyclist's paradise, but there are important restrictions. Bicycles are not allowed on hiking trails, and cyclists must respect one-way directions on motor roads. Bicycling is permitted on all paved park roads and on all carriage roads (for more information on the carriage road system, see chapter 1, Acadia National Park: A Visitor's Overview), except private carriage roads that are so posted. Please respect the wishes of private carriage road owners. Failure to do so may jeopardize all public use of the private roads.

In addition, bicyclists using the park's carriage roads must abide by the National Park Service's "Rules of the Road":

- Stay to the right. Pass carefully on the left.
- Yield to others. Do not obstruct the carriage road. Move to the side when stopping or taking a break.
- Be prepared to stop. Stay in control.
- Gravel surfaces are loose, and quick stops are dangerous.
- Speeding is discourteous and dangerous.
- Dress for the weather and carry water.
- Use a map.
- Wear a helmet. When approaching others from behind, call out or use your bell.
- Horses can be unpredictable. Stop and let them pass.

PROTECT THE SEALS

Each spring, harbor seals migrate to the rocky ledges and islands off Acadia National Park to raise their young and feed in the rich gulf waters. Seal pups are born in protected coves between mid-April and mid-June. Human curiosity poses a hazard for the pups. When boats or hikers approach the islands or ledges for a closer look, frightened seals jump into the water to escape. Under these stressful conditions, mother seals may abandon their pups, and young seals may find it impossible to return to the safety of the ledges.

To protect harbor seals, the park service has set forth the following "Boater Ethics":

- Give seal haul-out areas the widest berth possible. Researchers have observed seals panicked by kayaks up to 1 *mile* away.
- Retreat immediately if seals raise their necks or chests into the air, move toward the water, or enter the water. This behavior indicates that the seals are disturbed. Leave the area immediately, for your presence prolongs their stress.
- View seals from a discreet land location and at a distance, using binoculars or a spotting scope. Kayaks and canoes

disturb seals the most. Researchers theorize that seals retain genetic memories of being hunted by humans in kayaks and canoes, or that a kayaker's profile and slow pace may mimic a killer whale, one of their major predators.

PROTECT THE FALCONS

Every year since 1990, a pair of peregrine falcons has nested on the east side of Champlain Mountain. Since 1995, another pair of falcons has made a nest on Beech Cliffs. To protect this endangered species and give newborn falcon chicks the greatest likelihood of survival, the park service has seasonally closed the Precipice Trail and a loop trail at the top of Beech Cliffs. The park service urges all visitors to protect Acadia's falcons by staying off the closed trails. Visitors may observe the falcons from the parking area at the Precipice trailhead, located on the Park Loop Road. Most mornings in the summer and fall, a ranger or park volunteer sets up a telescope so that visitors can easily and safely view the falcons and their chicks.

A broken tree inspires a "limbo" game. But never *break or deface a living tree! It is against park regulations and may kill the tree.*

Watching harbor seals

LIGHT STOVES, NOT FIRES

Even in designated campgrounds where fires are allowed, the park service discourages wood fires and recommends portable cooking stoves. Fires rob forests of decomposing matter, present hazards in drought-stricken areas, and create haze in pristine skies. Also, ash carried by runoff contaminates lakes and streams. If you feel you cannot camp without a fire, make it small, do not use it for cooking, limit its duration, and extinguish it carefully.

PROTECT THE LAKES

Acadia's lakes and streams are fragile and easily damaged by careless visitors. To protect them, eliminate waste at least 200 feet away from all bodies of water. In addition, do not use any soaps in or near lakes and streams, because all soaps pollute, even those that claim to be biodegradable.

Also, many popular lakes within Acadia National Park are public drinking water reservoirs. Swimming is strictly prohibited at these lakes, and boating is prohibited within 1,000 feet of intake pipes. In the interest of public safety (and to avoid receiving an expensive citation), park visitors should abide by these restrictions.

Safety Tips for Acadia National Park

This section summarizes the basic precautions to be taken when visiting Acadia National Park. Be alert to the dangers described below and be prepared with the appropriate knowledge and gear to minimize hazardous situations. The checklist at the end of this section lists the essentials to take on every outing.

HYPOTHERMIA

Hypothermia is the lowering of the body's core temperature to a degree sufficient to cause illness. The condition is always serious and sometimes fatal. Signs of mild hypothermia include complaints of coldness, shivering, loss of coordination, and apathy. More severe hypothermia causes mental confusion, uncontrollable shivering, slurred speech, and a core temperature low enough to cause permanent damage or death.

Because small bodies lose heat more rapidly than large ones, children are more vulnerable to hypothermia than adults. Early signs of hypothermia in children may be crankiness and fussiness, which can also be caused by ordinary fatigue. A child may not even realize he or she is cold until serious shivering begins. Hikers, especially children, can become hypothermic when temperatures are well above freezing. Wind chill is a critical, and often overlooked, cause of hypothermia. Observe the following precautions:

- Carry an adequate supply of warm clothing, including wool sweaters, socks, gloves, and hats, to insulate against heat loss. Gloves, hats, and scarves are particularly effective because they protect areas that are especially sensitive to heat loss. Carry these items even when the weather looks warm and sunny. On cool, rainy days, avoid cotton clothing, which is not warm when wet and wicks warmth away from the body.
- Dress in layers and remove unneeded layers to prevent excessive sweating, which lowers body temperature through

evaporation. React quickly to temperature changes, whether occasioned by weather or changes in activity levels.
- Avoid excessive exposure to wind and rain. *Always* carry rain gear. Put on rain gear before you get wet.
- Carry food high in carbohydrates and sugar that the body can quickly convert to heat.
- Carry warm liquids, such as hot cocoa, when hiking in cold weather.
- Avoid resting against ice, snow, or cold rocks, which draw heat away from the body. Place an insulating barrier, such as a foam pad, between the body and cold surfaces.
- Cover the mouth with a wool scarf to warm air entering the lungs.

If a member of your group shows signs of hypothermia, stop and take immediate steps to warm the person. Promptness is particularly important when treating hypothermia in children. Add layers of clothing. Replace wet clothes with dry ones. If possible, administer warm liquids or food. If necessary, build a small fire to warm the victim and dry wet clothing. Holding a cold child close to your body while wrapping a parka or blanket around the two of you is particularly effective.

HEAT-RELATED ILLNESS

Hiking, biking, and paddling in warm weather, or in the open sun, can cause excessive loss of water and salts (electrolytes). Failure to replace water and electrolytes can lead to dehydration, heat exhaustion, or even heat stroke. To prevent heat-related illnesses, consume adequate amounts of water and electrolytes. Avoid salt tablets in favor of salted snacks and liquids, which you should always carry in amounts greater than you are likely to need. Flavored powders containing electrolytes may be added to water to replace those lost through perspiration. Remember that thirst is not a reliable indicator of the need for water. Schedule regular water stops to ensure against dehydration.

SUN EXPOSURE

Precautions against overexposure to the sun are necessary in any season. During the summer, it is particularly important to avoid excessive exposure, especially on summit hikes. Take additional precautions when in, on, or near the water, for radiation reflects off the water's surface.

LIGHTNING

If you are hiking on an open ridge or treeless summit during an electrical storm, you may be in danger of being hit by lightning, because lightning strikes at the highest object. Paddlers caught on the water during a storm may also be in danger, because water conducts electricity. If you do get caught in a thunderstorm in an unprotected area, take the following precautions:

- Boaters should return to the nearest shoreline as quickly as possible and wait out the storm on dry land. Keep away from puddles, streams, and other bodies of water.
- Do not seek shelter under natural features, such as lone or tall trees, rock overhangs, or large boulders, that project above their surroundings. Such large, exposed objects are more likely to be hit by lightning because of their height.
- Do *not* lie flat on the ground. This increases the body area exposed to electrical current in the event of a nearby strike.
- Assume the safest position—huddle on your knees with your head down. Crouch near medium-size boulders, if available.
- Safe places during thunderstorms include cars and large buildings; the larger, the better.
- If you are retreating to safety during a storm, stay as low as possible and remove children from back carriers.

Be aware of the fickleness of coastal weather. Storms can approach extremely rapidly. If you see a storm, the most prudent course is to retreat at once to a safe area. Most thunderstorms originate in the north or west and blow to the east or southeast. Do not proceed to a summit or remain on a body of water if you hear or see signs of an approaching electrical storm.

FOG

Dense fog may envelope summit hikers and boaters rapidly, unexpectedly, and in any season. It is therefore essential to carry a compass on all outings. If you find yourself in dense fog while hiking, be sure to locate the next cairn or blaze before leaving the last one. Boaters should keep an eye on their heading and be prepared to find and follow a back bearing if necessary to return to shore.

BOATING SAFETY

Maine law requires that all boats have an approved personal flotation device for each occupant. Furthermore, this book strenuously recommends that all occupants *wear* their life jackets due to the extremely cold temperatures of Maine waters (the ocean temperature rarely rises above 55 degrees F). It is very difficult and exhausting to put on a life jacket after capsizing.

Paddlers should also be cognizant of heavy boat traffic, especially in Frenchman Bay. Although small boats have the right-of-way, it essential to paddle defensively in the company of large commercial and recreational vessels.

DRINKING WATER—GIARDIASIS PREVENTION

Always carry a large quantity of safe drinking water—at least a quart per person. It is not safe to drink from any of the lakes and streams in the park. The waters may be infested with *Giardia lamblia,* a parasitic protozoa that wreaks havoc in the human digestive system. Giardia infestation is caused when mammals such as muskrats defecate in or near the water, or when water has been contaminated by the careless disposal of human waste. Symptoms of giardiasis in humans include diarrhea, abdominal distention, gas, and cramps. The symptoms appear 7 to 10 days after infection. If you suffer these symptoms, it is necessary to obtain treatment from a physician.

To purify water, boil it for 3 to 6 minutes. You may also disinfect the water chemically or by filtration, but these methods have not been proven as effective as heat. All water that might be swallowed, including water used for cooking, cleaning dishes, and brushing teeth, must be treated.

To help prevent the spread of giardiasis and other harmful diseases, dig temporary latrines at least 8 inches deep, 8 to 10 inches wide, and 200 feet away from water sources and trails. After use, fill the hole with loose soil and tap down lightly. Of course, campers should wash hands thoroughly after use of the latrine. Parents should teach children safe toileting practices to protect their health and to keep lakes, streams, and rivers clean.

BEACH-COMBING HAZARDS

The park's rocky shoreline can be hazardous to inattentive beachcombers. Hikers must take great care when crossing wet, slick surfaces and slippery seaweed-covered rocks. In addition, on stormy days, especially in the spring and fall, waves can catch walkers by surprise and even drag the unaware out to sea. Pay attention to your steps and to the incoming waves, and never let children stray.

Second, be aware of the tides when exploring coastal areas. Park and town newspapers print tide schedules daily. Check the tables before setting out across an intertidal zone to be sure that you do not get stranded.

Trees cut by beaver

TICKS

Ticks can transmit Lyme disease. The symptoms of Lyme disease in advanced cases are severe, including arthritis, meningitis, neurological problems, and cardiac symptoms. Symptoms can occur a few weeks to over a year after the tick bite. Early signs can include a rash around the infected tick bite and flulike symptoms. Timely diagnosis and treatment can cure or lessen the severity of the disease. If you or your family experiences any of these symptoms after a tick bite, immediately contact your physician. Tick bites have been reported in Acadia National Park. Thus it is prudent to take the following precautions:

- Use an insect repellent containing DEET or permethrin; spray on shoes and clothing, especially socks, pant legs and cuffs, and shirt sleeves and cuffs. Avoid direct application of

DEET to skin, for this potentially harmful chemical (diethyltoluamide) can be absorbed through the skin. DEET can also damage rayon, acetate, and spandex, but is safe on nylon, cotton, and wool. When buying DEET, choose a formula containing no more than 35 percent DEET. Tests have shown that this amount provides as much protection as formulas containing higher concentrations. In addition, there are several repellents formulated especially for children with much lower concentrations of the harmful pesticide.

- Tuck pants into boots, and button cuffs and collars.
- Wear light-colored clothing to spot ticks more easily.
- Check frequently for ticks on skin, scalp, and clothing. This may be done on rest breaks while hiking. Ticks often spend many hours on a body before they transmit the virus, so there is no need to panic if you find a tick. Infection can, nevertheless, be transmitted soon after the tick attaches, so it is prudent to check regularly.
- When visiting prime tick habitats—grassy, brushy areas from spring through midsummer—apply insect repellent, wear appropriate clothing, stay on trails, and increase the frequency of tick inspections.

If you should discover a tick, if it is not deeply imbedded, remove it using tweezers, pulling it straight out. It is important to remove all head and mouth parts to prevent infection. If it is deeply imbedded, covering it with kerosene will suffocate it and cause it to back out. After removing the tick, wash the area with soap and water. Although ticks are rare in late summer and fall, you should still check your family regularly.

LOST AND FOUND

The park's trails are generally well marked and easy to follow. At frequent intervals along most hiking trails, the park service has painted blue blazes on granite outcroppings and trailside trees. Cairns (piles of stones) also mark most summit trails. As an extra precaution, always carry current topographic maps for the area in which you are hiking. These maps are available at the park visitor center and at local outdoor supply stores and bookstores. Topographic trail maps are particularly useful because they show terrain features and elevation by means of contour lines.

Tidepooling is fun, but watch your step on the slippery algae!

If you have old maps, make sure they are up-to-date. Finally, buy waterproof maps, or carry the maps in a waterproof pouch.

Also, carry a reliable compass and know how to use it in conjunction with your topographic map. If you do not feel confident, check with outing clubs in your area for instruction. Good books providing instruction in compass use are also available (see appendix B, Recommended Reading).

Children are particularly vulnerable to getting lost and are less able to care for themselves if they do. When hiking or biking, do not let children stray from your sight. Take the following preventive measures to guard against potentially traumatic or dangerous situations:

- Teach children to stay with the group.
- Instruct children never to leave designated trails.
- Give children whistles, with strict instructions to use the whistles only when lost.
- Instruct children to remain in one place if they become lost. That way, they can be found more easily.
- If children must move while lost, teach them how to build "ducks" by placing a smaller stone on top of a larger stone. By leaving a trail of ducks, the child will more easily be found.

CLOTHING

Due to the Maine coast's changeable weather, always carry warm clothes and rain gear. Very cold and wet conditions can occur in the park at any time of year. Layers are best for warmth. Carry wool sweaters and rain ponchos or waterproof jackets and rain pants. Before your trip, test all seams for watertight seals, and reseal if necessary. If hiking in the spring, wear waterproof boots. Cotton sweatshirts are not recommended because they are useless when wet. Bring hats and gloves when hiking or biking in the spring and fall.

FIRST-AID KIT

Carry a first-aid kit on *every* outing. Commercially packaged kits are available in convenient sizes. If you purchase one, check its contents against the following list and supplement if necessary. To make your own first-aid kit, simply purchase the items listed below and place them in a nylon stuff bag, zippered container, or aluminum box.

- Adhesive bandage strips (bring an abundant supply; their psychological value to children cannot be underestimated)
- Butterfly bandages for minor lacerations
- Sterile gauze pads (4x4 inches) for larger wounds
- Adhesive tape to attach dressings
- Antibiotic ointment to treat wounds and cuts
- Moleskin™ for blisters
- Triangle bandages for slings
- Athletic tape for multiple uses
- Children's pain reliever
- Adult pain reliever

- Betadine swabs (povidone iodine) for an antiseptic
- Alcohol pads to cleanse skin
- Elastic bandage for sprains
- Knife with scissors and tweezers (for removing ticks and splinters)
- Space blanket for emergency warmth
- First-aid instruction booklet

Checklist for Safe Outings

Use the following checklist before departing on each of your outings. It includes the "Ten Essentials" compiled by The Mountaineers and adds a few extra "essentials" specific to the needs of children. Bringing the following items prepares you for emergencies due to weather, injuries, or other unforeseen circumstances.

THE TEN "PLUS" ESSENTIALS

1. Extra clothing. Though it means extra weight, it ensures against cold, cranky children and hypothermia.
2. Extra food and water. Extra food gives you energy to travel longer in emergencies.
3. Sunglasses. Hats with visors offer protection to youngsters too young to wear sunglasses.
4. Knife.
5. Firestarter candle or chemical fuel.
6. First-aid kit.
7. Matches in a waterproof container. Containers are available at outdoor supply stores, or use a 35mm film canister.
8. Flashlight. You will need a flashlight to negotiate trails at night or to prepare a camp at unexpected hours.
9. Map. Carry a current map in a waterproof case.
10. Compass. Know how to use it.
11. Sunscreen. Test for skin sensitivity before the trip.
12. Whistles. These are to be used only in the event children become lost.
13. Water purification tablets. The tablets ensure a source of emergency drinking water.
14. Bike repair kit. Know how to use it.
15. Bike helmets. Each rider and passenger must wear one.
16. Personal flotation devices. Take one for each boater.

17. Insect repellent. Necessary for comfortable outings and camping, particularly in the spring and early summer.

A Note about Safety

Safety is an important concern in all outdoor activities. No guidebook can alert you to every hazard or anticipate the limitations of every reader. Therefore, the descriptions of roads, trails, routes, and natural features in this book are not representations that a particular place or excursion will be safe for your party. When you follow any of the routes described in this book, you assume responsibility for your own safety. Under normal conditions, such excursions require the usual attention to traffic, road and trail conditions, weather, terrain, the capabilities of your party, and other factors. Keeping informed on current conditions and exercising common sense are the keys to a safe, enjoyable outing.

The Mountaineers

Paved Road		City or Town	o
Unpaved Road		Viewpoint	
Carriage Road		Building	
Secondary Carriage Road		Ranger Station	
Featured Trail		Camping	
Secondary Trail		Picnic Area	
Trailhead	Ⓣ	Bridge	
Parking	Ⓟ	Mountain Peak	▲
U.S. Highway	(1)	Wetlands/Marsh	
State/County Road	(198)	National Park Boundary	
Carriage Road Post Number	3		
Trip Number	3	Boat Launch	
River/Stream		Turnaround	

CHAPTER

1

Acadia National Park:
A Visitor's Overview

The essence of Acadia National Park is its sensational topography. In no other place within the continental United States do mountains rise so abruptly from the ocean shore. Within this glacier-carved landscape lies the only fjord in the contiguous United States. Lush forests cover the park's valleys and mountainsides, and clear lakes and ponds nestle below its bare granite peaks. And all around this beautiful island, an ocean full of sealife ebbs and flows, laps and crashes, in constant motion against the rugged, rocky coastline.

Although the park's beauty is indisputable and readily apparent to the most casual sightseer, the real treasures of Acadia require a bit of effort to uncover. Visiting families can rejoice, nevertheless, because Acadia National Park provides superlative access to its natural wonders. Due to its small size and extensive network of roads, it is one of the easiest national parks to enjoy and explore.

Just what is waiting for adventuresome families? In five areas, Acadia National Park absolutely excels. Consider Acadia's many offerings.

Hiking Trails: Family-Size Challenges

Acadia's bare-topped summits, all under 1,600 feet, offer unique opportunities for young hikers to reach glorious peaks in only a few hours' hike. In no other park can hikers find such exquisitely

A shoreline hike

engineered trails. Hikers of all ages can ascend steps of granite painstakingly built into the mountainside, and scale sheer cliffs with the aid of iron handholds and ladders. The park's 120 miles of trails offer an incredibly wide range of family hiking experiences.

Carriage Roads: Carefree Biking and Strolling

An impressive network of carriage roads traverse the park. On these 57 miles of broad, view-filled roads, families can bike, stroll, or even ride horseback free from the pressures of automobile traffic. Visitors can thank John D. Rockefeller, Jr. for the superb carriage road system. Not only did Rockeller donate nearly a third of the land for Acadia National Park, he also masterminded and funded the carriage roads that traverse the eastern portion of the park. Rockefeller's philosophy was to provide visitors with nonmotorized access to the exquisite vistas, waterfalls, mountains, and forests of the park in a manner that respects and preserves the natural landscape. According to his instructions, only native plants were used as roadside plantings, and a minimum of trees were removed to enhance the views from the road. His sixteen magnificent, hand-cut granite bridges were designed to follow the contours of the land, and one was even redesigned so that ancient hemlock trees would be spared. Built between 1917 and 1933, the carriage road system is even more important today, as automobile traffic predictably intrudes on the quiet enjoyment of nature on Mount Desert Island. The carriage roads provide an effective and beautiful sanctuary, offering unparalleled family cycling.

Ocean Exploring: Variety and Accessibility

Most of Acadia National Park is located on Mount Desert Island, a small island off the Atlantic coast that is only 18 miles long and 14 miles wide. From every peak in the park and from most trails and carriage roads, visitors experience the sights, sounds, and smells of the sea. Visitors never seem to tire watching the comings and goings of hundreds of seabirds, mammals, lobster boats, and sailing vessels. Like most of Acadia National Park, the ocean and shore are easily accessible. The park provides families with myriad opportunities to enjoy, study, and explore the sea, from whale watching, sea kayaking, and puffin cruises to quiet tide pooling and beach-combing. Especially for visitors from landlocked places, the sea is full of variety, surprises, and mystery.

In addition, two sections of Acadia National Park that are not located on Mount Desert Island provide families with especially intimate encounters with the ocean environment. The **Schoodic Peninsula** lies about 45 miles northeast of Mount Desert Island via automobile and offers a pristine and isolated Maine coast experience. Visitors can explore in solitude its rocky shore, offshore islands, and untamed forests. To explore a beautiful and undeveloped offshore island, visit Acadia's **Isle au Haut.** Accessible by mail boat from Stonington (about 60 miles southwest of Mount Desert Island), Isle au Haut is not easy to reach, but the rewards are terrific hiking trails, splendid isolation, and superlative ocean-view campsites. For more information on both the Schoodic Peninsula and Isle au Haut, see chapter 4.

Forests and Waterways: Full of Wonder

Acadia's well-maintained hiking trails and carriage roads lead families effortlessly into the park's rich forests and lovely waterways. At Acadia, the coniferous North Woods overlaps with the colorful deciduous forest of the Temperate Zone. The result is a beautiful patchwork of diversity, providing homes for over 300 species of birds, numerous small mammals, amphibians, reptiles, wildflowers, and an amazing assortment of fungi, mosses, ferns, and lichens. Often surrounded by forest, the park's many streams, lakes, and ponds provide gentle spaces for family paddling, fishing, and swimming.

Park Programs Extraordinaire

Acadia National Park offers families an extraordinary array of interpretive programs. Although all national parks provide interpretive services, the depth and variety at Acadia are truly outstanding. From bird-watching expeditions at dawn to campground slide programs each evening, the daily choices are rich and appealing. Whether the subject is history, geology, oceanography, or zoology, visitors are likely to find programs that fit their interests. Best of all, there are many activities specifically designed for families that introduce children to the forest, seashore, and hiking. Most of these invaluable programs are offered free of charge.

Planning Your Trip Is Essential

For those visiting Acadia National Park between July Fourth and Labor Day, camping or lodging reservations are highly advisable. Three million visitors descend on the park each summer, so it is not unusual for all rooms and campsites to be booked on Mount Desert Island. To plan your visit, read the following sections and decide when, how, and where you want to go. Write or call the park to request maps and information and contact the appropriate chamber of commerce to receive information on lodging. Information is also available at www.nps.gov/acad. Those wishing to camp should make reservations at the campground of their choice. With these basic preparations in place, families can arrive at Acadia worry-free and ready to devote all their energy to exploration and enjoyment.

IMPORTANT ADDRESSES AND PHONE NUMBERS

Acadia National Park, P.O. Box 177,
Bar Harbor, ME 04609; (207) 288-3338 visitor center,
288-3369 or 288-3360 emergency assistance,
www.nps.gov/acad
Bar Harbor Chamber of Commerce, P.O. Box 158,
Bar Harbor, ME 04609; (207)
288-2404 summer or (800) 288-5103 winter
Mount Desert–Northeast Harbor Chamber of Commerce,
(207) 276-5040 summer
Southwest Harbor Tremont Chamber of Commerce,
(207) 244-9264 or (800) 423-9464

HOW TO GET THERE

By air: The Bar Harbor/Hancock County Airport, Acadia's near-est airport, is located 12 miles from Bar Harbor and is served by Colgan Air (207-667-7171 or 1-800-272-5488). Bangor International Airport (approximately 50 miles away) is the closest major airport and Portland International Jetport (164 miles away) is served by several major airlines. Taxi service to Mount Desert Island is available from the Bar Harbor/Hancock County and Bangor International Airports (207-667-5995 and 207-223-4070).

Rental cars: Rental cars are available at the Bar Harbor/ Hancock County and Bangor International Airports.

By car: Acadia National Park is adjacent to the town of Bar Harbor and is easily accessible by car. From Bangor, drive US 1A south to Ellsworth, then follow Route 3 south to Bar Harbor. From Boston and Portland, drive north on Interstate 95 to Bangor, then follow the directions above from Bangor.

Driving distances: The distances to Acadia National Park (Mount Desert Island) from the nearest major cities are: 56 miles from Bangor; 164 miles from Portland; 270 miles from Boston; 356 miles from Montreal, Canada; 475 miles from New York City; and 700 miles from Washington, D.C.

By bus: Greyhound/Vermont Transit offers bus service be-tween Boston and Bar Harbor from mid-June to Labor Day (207-772-6587). Downeast Transportation provides year-round service

Crossing a brook—carefully—on a log bridge

between Bar Harbor and Ellsworth and around Mount Desert Island (207-667-5796). There is also shuttle service from the Bangor International Airport to Bar Harbor (207-223-4070).

Public transportation within the park: To help reduce congestion, pollution, and parking problems, use the Island Explorer, a free, propane-powered shuttle bus that links hotels, inns, campgrounds, and trailheads throughout Acadia National Park. With the ability to transport cyclists, bikes and hikers, the Island Explorer buses make possible a wide range of one-way hiking and biking trips. The shuttle operates daily, late June through early September (207-288-4573 or www.exploreacadia.com).

WHEN TO GO

Spring (May-June): Mid-May through June is considered pre-season. As in any season on Maine's coast, the weather is highly changeable, with periods of rain, sun, and fog. Daytime temperatures average in the 50s and 60s. Although the trails and campgrounds are less crowded and the days are blissfully long, biting blackflies can make outings miserable from approximately late May to mid-June. These flies try the patience of the hardiest campers, so be prepared.

Summer (July-August): Summer is high tourist season, with an accompanying rise in prices and park attendance. During July and August, daytime high temperatures generally range between 70 and 80 degrees F. Peak mosquito season persists through July. An assortment of wildflowers and fascinating fungi, ferns, and lichen grace meadows, summits, and open woodlands.

In August, biting bugs begin to retreat noticeably, although mooseflies and deerflies may still be a problem in some areas. Days are still warm and nights are usually comfortably brisk. Flowers bloom and a sumptuous assortment of blueberries, huckleberries, and raspberries ripens in all corners of the park.

Cold, wet weather can arrive unexpectedly, even in July and August. To cope with the changeable weather, visitors should dress in layers and always have rain gear handy.

Fall (September-October): Early autumn is exquisite, with the arrival of crisp weather and dramatic fall foliage. Peak fall colors generally arrive in the last week of September and first week of October. Autumn daytime temperatures return to the 50s and 60s. Nights can be cold. Rain is common in both months. In November, the winter season arrives.

WHERE TO STAY

Lodging

Although there is no lodging within Acadia National Park proper, there is a wide range of accommodations near the park on Mount Desert Island, from rustic campgrounds to elegant historic inns. During July and August and peak fall foliage weekends, it is highly advisable to make reservations. Much of the lodging on Mount Desert Island can be found in the bustling town of Bar Harbor. Helpful information on lodging (and restaurants and outfitters) is available free of charge from the Bar Harbor Chamber of Commerce.

Additional lodging is found in the quaint and quiet towns of Northeast Harbor and Southwest Harbor. Because these towns are both considerably smaller than Bar Harbor, they contain far fewer commercial establishments and offer a more limited range of accommodations and services. For information on accommodations in these towns, contact their chambers of commerce (see p. 35).

For lodging and campground information near the Schoodic Peninsula and Isle au Haut, write the Winter Harbor Chamber of

Commerce (Winter Harbor, ME 04693 for the Schoodic Peninsula) or call the Deer Isle/Stonington Chamber of Commerce (207-348-6124) for accommodations near Isle au Haut.

Camping

Campgrounds within Acadia National Park: The park service runs two campgrounds on Mount Desert Island in Acadia National Park: **Blackwoods Campground,** located 5 miles south of Bar Harbor, and **Seawall Campground,** located 4 miles south of Southwest Harbor. Both are in wooded settings within a short walk to the ocean. Both provide comfort stations, cold running water, dump stations, picnic tables, and fire rings. Neither has utility hook-ups. Hot showers and camp stores are available within 0.5 mile of both. Campers may reserve sites at Blackwoods up to five months in advance through National Park Reservation System, P.O. Box 1600, Cumberland, MD 21502; 1-800-365-2267).

Blackwoods is open year-round, with limited facilities in the off-season. Seawall Campground is open on a first-come, first-served basis from late May until late September only. During late July and August, the campground is usually full to capacity, and new campers must arrive very early in the morning for the chance to secure a campsite when departing campers check out. Both campgrounds also offer group campsites for educational and formally organized groups. To reserve a group campsite at either campground, write the park service to request a reservation form.

Both campgrounds provide a nice setting for family tent camping. Each evening, rangers present slide programs at campground amphitheaters. Seawall's location, across from a fine picnic area and dramatic sweep of rocky shoreline, is especially attractive. Hiking trails are convenient to both. The overall map at the beginning of this book shows the location of both campgrounds.

The third park service campground in Acadia National Park is the **Duck Harbor Campground**, located on the remote island of Isle au Haut, accessible by mail boat from Stonington. The small campground consists of five lean-to shelters, each providing breathtaking views of the ocean in a lovely wooded setting.

Between May 15 and October 15, campers can reserve the lean-tos, and usually reservations must be made far in advance for these exquisite sites. To make a reservation, apply in person at park headquarters or send a reservation request postmarked April 1 or later to Acadia National Park (attention: Isle au Haut

Bridge in historic Somesville

Reservations). Print your name, address, and telephone number, and the number of people in your party, along with your choice of dates. Due to high demand for campsites, campers are more likely to receive a reservation confirmation if alternative dates are given. You must send $25 with each reservation request. If the National Park Service is not able to honor the reservation, it will return the money. For additional information, you can call the park service, although it does not accept telephone requests for reservations.

Visiting Isle au Haut is a surprisingly complicated affair. Hikers must travel to the island by a mail boat from Stonington. There is no auto ferry, and there is no service to or from Isle au Haut on postal holidays (i.e., Memorial Day, Fourth of July, Labor Day). Before submitting a campground reservation request, campers should contact the Isle au Haut Ferry Company (Stonington, ME, 04681; 207-367-5193) for the boat schedule. Round-trip boat fares are approximately $20 for adults and $10 for children.

Backcountry campsites: Due to the small size and fragility of Acadia's backcountry, overnight camping is permitted only in the designated campgrounds described above. Off-trail backcountry camping is prohibited within the park.

Private campgrounds: Mount Desert Island hosts numerous private campgrounds, of varying nature and quality. In the list of private campgrounds found below, all are located on Mount Desert Island unless noted otherwise. When making camping reservations, call ahead to inquire about the facilities. Many of the private campgrounds cater to large recreational vehicles.

- Barcadia Campground, RFD 1, Box 2165, Bar Harbor, ME 04609; (207) 288-3520; 200 sites
- Bar Harbor Campground, Rte. 3, Bar Harbor, ME 04609; (207) 288-5185; 300 sites
- Bass Harbor Campground, Box 122, Bass Harbor, ME 04653; (207) 244-5857; 130 sites
- Hadley's Point Campground, RFD 1, Box 1790, Bar Harbor, ME 04609; (207) 288-4808; 180 sites
- Mount Desert Campground, Rte. 198, Somesville, ME 04660; (207) 244-3710; 153 sites (excellent for tents)
- Mount Desert Narrows Campground, Rte. 3, Bar Harbor, ME 04609; (207) 288-3520; 239 sites
- Narrows Too Camping Resort, Rte. 3, Trenton, ME 04605; (207) 667-4300; 110 sites

The downeast charm of a lobster shack in Seal Harbor

- Ocean Wood (Schoodic Peninsula), P.O. Box 111, Birch Harbor, ME 04613; (207) 963-7194; 70 sites
- Quietside Campground, P.O. Box 8, West Tremont, ME 04690; (207) 244-5992; 35 sites
- Somes Sound View Campground, Hall Quarry, ME 04660; (207) 244-3890; 60 sites
- Spruce Valley Campground, Rte. 102, Bar Harbor, ME 04609; (207) 288-5139; 100 sites
- The White Birches Campground, Southwest Harbor, ME 04679; (207) 244-3739; 60 sites

Emergency Medical Services

If a medical emergency should arise while you are in Acadia National Park, call the park service (288-3369 or 288-3360 for emergency assistance). In Bar Harbor, call 911. Mount Desert Island Hospital, located in Bar Harbor, provides 24-hour emergency care (207-288-5081). Medical facilities are also available at the Southwest Harbor Medical Center (207-244-5513) and the Northeast Harbor Medical Center (207-276-3331). Eastern Maine Medical Center (207-973-7000), the region's largest hospital, is located in Bangor.

Family Activities within Acadia National Park and Nearby

YOUR FIRST STOP: Acadia National Park Visitor Center

The quickest way to learn about family activities within Acadia National Park is to stop at the Hulls Cove Visitor Center located just off Route 3 at the start of Park Loop Road, north of the town of Bar Harbor. At the visitor center, you will receive a park map and a *Beaver Log* (the park service publication listing the month's activities) and meet a helpful staff of park rangers. Families can also view a short film on Acadia in the center's auditorium, check out an awesome relief map of the park, and purchase books and maps. The book shop has a particularly nice selection of books for children and young naturalists. The visitor center is open daily from May 1 through October 31, 8:00 A.M. to 4:30 P.M.

NATIONAL PARK SERVICE INTERPRETIVE PROGRAMS

From June to October, park service ranger-naturalists run an extraordinary program of guided walks, boat tours, natural history lectures, evening slide shows, and campfire talks. Most are offered free of charge, and many are geared for children. Whether your family's interests run to flora, fauna, geology, or history, there is likely to be a program that fills the bill. If you have young children, do not be afraid to try a ranger-led hike. Often there are other families with children attending, and the children can bond with each other while the parents listen and learn. Please note that reservations for popular ranger-led activities are required in peak season. For a complete schedule of park activities, inquire at the visitor center. As mentioned above, Acadia's schedule of activities is published in the park's monthly newsletter, the *Beaver Log*. Daily programs are also listed in *Acadia Weekly*, a free weekly publication widely available at chambers of commerce, hotels and motels, and stores in surrounding communities. For more information on park service naturalist activities and to make reservations, call (207) 288-5262.

Acadia National Park also offers a **Junior Ranger** program for children 8 and older. To become a junior ranger, children must attend at least two interpretive programs and must complete a fun workbook about the park. Junior rangers earn a handsome pin and much satisfaction. Inquire at the visitor center for details.

MUSEUMS OF ACADIA NATIONAL PARK AND MOUNT DESERT ISLAND

Please note that the museum hours listed below indicate peak-season hours (late June to Labor Day). More restricted hours may apply in the off season.

Within Acadia National Park

Abbe Museum of Stone Age Antiquities explores the life of Maine's prehistoric inhabitants through a collection of ancient artifacts and illustrative dioramas. Children can examine prehistoric pottery, stone-age tools, and a birch-bark canoe, and can even enter a wigwam. Watch for children's programs such as the "Mystery Dig" where children can experience hands-on archaeology. Open daily, 10:00 A.M. to 4:00 P.M. Located in the park's Sieur de Monts area. Small admission fee (207-288-3519).

The Nature Center of Acadia National Park examines the park's natural history in an intimate kid-size setting. Exhibits cover fire ecology, beaver activity, air pollution, and the survival of endangered species. Open daily, 9:00 A.M. to 5:00 P.M. Located at Sieur de Monts. Free admission.

Islesford Historical Museum on Little Cranberry Island quaintly illustrates the lives of the early settlers of the Cranberry Isles and their seafaring culture through annotated displays of historical artifacts. Accessible by mail boat or tour boat (see Table 1, Boat Trips and Ferries from Mount Desert Island). Open daily, 10:30 A.M. to 12:00 A.M. and 12:30 P.M. to 4:30 P.M. Free admission.

Outside Acadia National Park

The Natural History Museum is filled with dioramas of mammals, birds, and sea life of coastal Maine. The museum also offers a hands-on discovery room and a short self-guided nature trail. Located at the College of the Atlantic, on Route 3 in Bar Harbor. Open daily, 9:00 A.M. to 5:00 P.M. Small admission fee (207-288-5015).

The Oceanarium operates three uniquely intriguing facilities on Mount Desert Island where visitors can explore and learn about different aspects of Maine's coastal environment. All are open daily, 9:00 A.M. to 5:00 P.M., except Sundays. In addition, the Oceanarium/Lobster Hatchery offers evening hours.

Oceanarium / Bar Harbor provides a large wetland setting in which visitors can take a guided tour along the Thomas Bay marsh walk and visit an observation tower to view shorebirds. Inside the facility, guests can meet a genuine lobsterman and board a real lobster boat. Located on Route 3 at Thomas Bay. Admission fee (207-288-5005).

Oceanarium / Lobster Hatchery presents 5,000 to 10,000 tiny lobsters in a small but fascinating working lobster hatchery. A tour guide explains the life cycle of lobsters and the role of hatcheries. Open evenings as well as days in July and August (call for hours), this is a great after-dinner activity. Located at One Harbor Place (the town dock) in Bar Harbor. Admission fee (207-288-2334).

Oceanarium / Southwest Harbor offers wonderful hands-on exhibits exploring the sea life of coastal Maine. Touch, smell, listen, and learn amid a wealth of interactive exhibits, including twenty tanks filled with sea creatures. Located on Clark Point Road in Southwest Harbor, between the Coast Guard Base and Beal's Lobster Wharf. Admission fee (207-244-7330).

Wendell Gilley Museum features intricate wooden bird carvings by the master Wendell Gilley in a beautiful building. Children enjoy the live carving demonstrations. Located on Route 102 in Southwest Harbor. Open Tuesday through Sunday, 10:00 A.M. to 4:00 p.m. Admission fee (207-244-7555).

Historical Society Museum houses artifacts, photographs, clothing, and tools of the early settlers of Mount Desert Island. Located in the Jesup Memorial Library, 34 Mount Desert Street, Bar Harbor. Open Monday through Saturday, 1:00 P.M. to 4:00 P.M. Free admission, but small donations appreciated (207-288-4245).

Mount Desert Historical Society Museum highlights early life in picturesque Somesville. Located on Route 102 at Oak Hill Road in Somesville. Open Wednesdays and Sundays, 2:00 p.m. to 5:00 p.m. Free admission; donations appreciated.

Wooden decoy carving at the Wendell Gilley Museum

Great Harbor Collection houses artifacts of the early settlers. Located on Route 198 in Northeast Harbor. Open daily except Sunday (call for hours). Free admission, but donations gladly accepted (207-276-5262).

BOAT TRIPS

Sea cruising is a wonderful way to see exciting marine life as well as the dramatic topography of Mount Desert Island. The choices are many, from whale-watching excursions and sunset schooner sails to guided kayak tours. On all boating expeditions, be sure to dress warmly (layers are best) and bring binoculars. In peak season, reservations are necessary for all outings. For a comparative listing of all boat tours, see Table 1, Boat Trips and Ferries from Mount Desert Island.

National Park Boat Cruises

On the following three boat cruises, national park naturalists accompany passengers and provide rich and entertaining natural history interpretation.

The Baker Island Cruise tours rugged Baker Island. Land with a park ranger by small boat and explore the island on a moderate, guided hike. The outing lasts about 4.5 hours and leaves from the municipal pier in Northeast Harbor (207-276-3717).

The Frenchman Bay Nature Cruise tours Frenchman Bay in search of ospreys, eagles, and porpoises for approximately 2 hours. Meet at Whalewatcher, Inc., next to the municipal pier in Bar Harbor (207-288-3322).

The Islesford Historical Cruise goes to Little Cranberry Island and the historic town of Islesford. Learn about the human and natural history of the area, then land and tour the quaint town of Islesford by foot, including the Islesford Historical Museum. The trip takes about 2.75 hours and leaves from the municipal pier in Northeast Harbor (207-276-5352).

Whale Watching

Whale-watching cruises are a favorite family activity for park visitors. The Gulf of Maine is an excellent place for sighting humpback, fin, right, and minke whales. Cruises usually last about 4 hours. Be prepared for cool to cold weather (the offshore temperature is often 20 degrees cooler than onshore) and for some rough water. Bring binoculars for best viewing. Consult Table 1, Boat Trips and Ferries from Mount Desert Island, for information on the many cruise companies operating out of Bar Harbor. Reservations are advisable.

Naturalist Sea Cruises

The waters surrounding Acadia National Park are also rich in smaller sea life and are an excellent place to view harbor seals, porpoises, puffins, eagles, osprey, and other seabirds. Choose from a variety of naturalist cruises, usually about 2 hours long. Three cruises include narration by a park naturalist (see National Park Boat Cruises, above). Consult Table 1, Boat Trips and Ferries from Mount Desert Island, for information on specific cruise companies. Reservations are recommended.

Sailing

A few companies offer visitors the opportunity to sail on beautiful and historic wooden sailing vessels. The schooners sail daily out of Bar Harbor and Northeast Harbor on 2-hour, half-day, full-day, or sunset sails. Check Table 1, Boat Trips and Ferries from Mount Desert Island, for more information.

Guided Kayak Tours

Another superlative family option is to take a guided kayak tour off the coast of Mount Desert Island. Paddle leisurely in stable, two-person kayaks while looking for wildlife. A guided trip is an excellent introduction to sea kayaking for children over 8 years. A variety of trips are offered by the following outfitters: Coastal Kayaking Tours, 106 Cottage St., Bar Harbor (207-288-9605 or 1-800-526-8615); National Park Sea Kayak Tours, 39 Cottage St., Bar Harbor (207-288-0342); Island Adventures, 141 Cottage St., Bar Harbor; Loon Bay Kayak, Route 3, Trenton (207-266-8888).

Boat Rentals

One of the best ways to experience Acadia National Park is to canoe or kayak in one of its many ponds or along its rocky ocean shoreline. Escape the crowds, do a little fishing, or pull up by some sun-warmed rocks to take a swim. Most of the boat rental companies listed below require renters to transport boats via car, and reservations are recommended.

- Acadia Outfitters. Canoe and sea kayak rentals with car-top carriers provided. Located at 106 Cottage Street, Bar Harbor (207-288-8118).
- Harbor Boat Rentals. Rents 13-foot and 17-foot Boston Whaler power boats only. Located at 1 West Street, Bar Harbor (207-288-3757).
- King Camping Supplies. Full-day or half-day canoe and car carrier rentals. Located adjacent to Seawall Campground on Route 102, Seawall Road, Manset (207-244-7006).
- Mansell Boat Company. Rents canoes, keel sailboats, and powerboats. Sailing lessons available. Located at Hinckley Yacht Yard, Southwest Harbor (207-244-5625).
- National Park Canoe Rental. Full-day and half-day canoe rentals conveniently located at Long Pond, the largest lake in the park. Put-in is directly across the street; no car transport is required. Fully equipped fishing canoe also available. Reservations recommended. Located on Route 102, directly across from the north end of Long Pond (207-244-5854).

Table 1
Boat Trips and Ferries from Mount Desert Island

NOTE: A cruise company may run several different trips offering different amenities. It is always advisable to call ahead for reservations and to inquire about specific cruise features before booking.

KEY: Ferry Service (**F**); Fishing and/or Lobstering (**Fish**); Nature Cruises (**N**); Sailing (**S**); Seabird Watching (**B**); NPS Interpreter (**NPS**); Seal Watching (**Seal**); Sunset Cruise (**Sun**); Whale Watching (**W**); Length of Cruise/Special Features (**L/SF**)

Cruise Company	F	Fish	N	S	B	NPS	Seal	Sun	W	L/SF
Acadia Cruises, Southwest Harbor, (207) 244-7399			X		X		X	X	X	3 2-hr trips daily/ video of underwater sea life
Acadian Whale Watcher, Bar Harbor, (207) 288-9794, (207) 288-9776, (800) 421-3307							X	X	X	3 4- to 5-hr trips (whale watch) daily July & August
Bar Harbor Whale Watch, Bar Harbor, (207) 288-2386		X	X		X		X	X	X	2 to 3 hrs (whale watch) 2 hrs (puffin cruise); 2 hrs (nature/seal cruise); 2.5 hrs (fishing)

Company								Description
Beal & Bunker, Northeast Harbor Town Pier, (207) 244-3575	X							6 1.5-hr trips daily to Cranberry Isles/mail boat ferry service
Blackjack, Northeast Harbor, (207) 288-3056, (207) 276-5043					X			4 1.5-hr trips daily; half-day & full-day trips by reservation/33-ft sloop, 6 passengers max
Bluenose Ferry, Route 3, Bar Harbor, (207) 288-3395	X							6- to 7-hr ferry service to Nova Scotia late June to mid-October
Cranberry Cove Boating Company, Southwest Harbor, (207) 244-5882	X			X				6 1.5-hr trips daily to Cranberry Isles/mail boat ferry service, historic wooden boat
Downeast Windjammer Cruises, Bar Harbor, (207) 288-4585, (207) 288-2373		X	X	X	X			9 1.5- & 2.5-hr trips daily; schooner, lighthouse, island cruises; motor cruise to Schoodic Point
Great Harbor Charters, Northeast Harbor, (207) 276-5352					X			half-day & full-day trips/33-ft sloop, 6 passengers max
Island Cruises, Bass Harbor, (207) 244-5785	X	X	X	X		X		2 2- to 3.5-hr trips daily/lunch cruise to Frenchboro

Cruise Company	L/SF	W	Sun	Seal	NPS	B	S	N	Fish	F
Isle au Haut Company, Stonington, (207) 367-5193, (207) 367-2355	daily ferry service to Isle au Haut (except mail holidays)									X
Islesford Ferry, Northeast Harbor, Town Pier, (207) 276-3717	2- to 4.5-hr cruise to Cranberry & Baker Islands/narration by NPS ranger		X	X	X	X		X		
Masako Queen, Northeast and Southwest Harbor, (207) 288-5927	2 5-hr trips daily/deep-sea fishing; no children under 5			X					X	
MDI Water Taxi, Northeast Harbors, (207) 244-7312	custom cruises by advance reservation			X		X	X	X		
Rachel B. Jackson, Manset Town Dock, (207) 244-7813	2.5 hrs/67-ft schooner, windjammer, full-moon cruises		X				X			
Sea Bird Watcher Company, Bar Harbor, Golden Anchor Pier, (207) 288-2025, (800) 247-3794	2-2.5 hrs (puffin cruise); 3.5-4 hrs (whale watch); 1.5-2 hrs (nature/sunset cruise)	X	X	X		X		X		

Sea Princess, Northeast Harbor, Town Pier, (207) 276-5352	2–3 hrs (nature cruise); 1.5 hrs (Somes Sound cruise); 3-hr dinner cruise to Little Cranberry Island
Sea Venture Custom Boat Tours, Bar Harbor, (207) 288-3355	Personalized private boat tours by naturalist/20-ft motor launch, 6 passengers max; wildlife sightseeing and island exploration
Swans Island Ferry, Bass Harbor, (207) 244-3254	6 40-min trips daily to Swans Island; 1 trip weekly to Frenchboro
Atlantis Whale Watcher, Bar Harbor, (207) 288-3322, (800) 508-1499	4 hrs (whale watch); shorter (nature, seal watch, lobster fishing cruises); schooner trips/NPS interpreter on some trips

BIKING

Acadia National Park is a superb place for family biking. Fifty-seven miles of carriage roads within the park offer scenic, challenging, and auto-free cycling. For those families who need to rent bikes, consult the list below. In peak season, reservations are advisable, especially if you need to rent child trailers, children's bikes, or trailer bikes (an attachment designed for children ages 4 to 8 that converts an adult bike to a tandem bicycle). All of the following outlets rent men's and women's mountain bikes.

Acadia Bike and Canoe. Rents children's bikes, tandem bikes, child seats, child trailers, and trailer bikes. 28 Cottage Street, Bar Harbor (207-288-9605 or 1-800-526-8615).

Acadia Outfitters. Rents children's bikes, tandem bikes, child seats, child trailers, and trailer bikes. 106 Cottage Street, Bar Harbor (207-288-8118).

Bar Harbor Bicycle Shop. Rents child seats, tandem bikes, and child trailers. 141 Cottage Street, Bar Harbor (207-288-3886).

Northeast Harbor Bike Shop. Rents children's bikes and tandems. Small shop; call for availability. Route 198, Northeast Harbor (207-276-5480).

Southwest Cycle. Rents children's bikes, child seats, and child trailers. Main Street, Southwest Harbor (207-244-5856 or 1-800-649-5856, in Maine only).

SWIMMING: ACADIA'S BEACHES AND PONDS

Despite its many miles of shoreline and numerous lakes and ponds, good swimming spots are at a premium in Acadia National Park. On a hot summer's day, here are your best bets.

Sand Beach is Acadia's only stretch of sandy ocean beach, and it is a gem. Its coarse sand is composed primarily of crushed shells and is a delightful composite of purple, pink, beige, green, and gray. The setting is gorgeous and the only drawback is the icy water. Most find it too cold for actual swimming, but children of all ages have fun playing in the waves. Changing rooms, rest rooms, and lifeguards provided. No dogs, please. On Park Loop Road, 0.3 mile after the park entrance station (see trip 1, Great Head Trail).

Seal Harbor Town Beach. This rocky beach offers changing rooms, rest rooms, and a float just offshore at high tide. A

Sand play at Echo Lake Beach

delightful lobster shack (also offering child-pleasing burgers, ice cream, and lemonade) is just a short walk away at the scenic Seal Harbor Town Pier. At Seal Harbor, off Route 3.

Echo Lake Beach is an excellent place to take young children for a real swim. Children love the temperate water and sandy beach. The only drawback is the midsummer crowds—the large parking lot is often filled to capacity by 11:00 A.M. Lifeguard, rest rooms, and changing rooms provided. No dogs, please. At the south end of Echo Lake, off Route 102, about 3.6 miles south of Somesville.

Upper Echo Lake. Older children enjoy the large rock ledges on the eastern shore of Echo Lake. To reach the ledges, park in the Acadia Mountain parking lot and descend on the short path through the woods. The Acadia Mountain parking lot is on Route 102, 3.1 miles south of Somesville.

Pond's End, North End of Long Pond. This small beach at the north end of Acadia's largest lake offers a small protected swimming area, clean, temperate water, and an offshore float. The beach provides easy access for small children and a grassy area for picnicking. Canoes can be rented on-site. At Long Pond on Route 102 (see trip 34, Long (Great) Pond).

53

Duck Rock at Long Pond. Long Pond is the drinking water reservoir for Southwest Harbor, and swimming is strictly prohibited near the pumping station at its south end. To reach the swimming area at Duck Rock, from the south end of Long Pond, take the easy path along the west side of the pond, and walk approximately 0.7 mile until you reach a prominent flat rock ledge, called Duck Rock. If this spot is occupied, there are some more good rocks a few hundred yards further north along the trail. To reach the south end of Long Pond and the west shore trail, see directions for trip 14, Mansell Mountain and map on p. 171.

The Bowl. This little mountain lake is beautiful, graced by warm water, gorgeous views, and even a couple of beaver lodges. Large rocks along the Bowl's east shore provide excellent swimming access. This tarn is accessible by a moderate 1.7-mile hike along the Gorham Trail or after a strenuous climb up the Beehive from Sand Beach (see trips 3, The Beehive Loop, and 4, Gorham Mountain and the Bowl Loop).

Sargent Mountain Pond. This small pond is only accessible by a fairly strenuous but beautiful hike. Hot and sweaty hikers will rejoice in the cool temperatures of this spring-fed pond. Large, flat rocks at its south end are inviting for both swimming and picnicking. Hike 1.8 miles from Jordan Pond (see trip 8, Penobscot and Sargent Mountains).

Lake Wood. This 16-acre, tree-lined pond is a pretty place for a summer swim. Its shallow water warms nicely and its gravelly bottom provides pleasant wading. Since it is easily accessible by car and near Bar Harbor, it is a popular swimming spot for locals. Find Lake Wood by driving north from Bar Harbor on Route 3, then turn left onto Crooked Road at Hulls Cove. Drive 1.1 miles west on Crooked Road, then turn left onto an unmarked road and drive 0.35 mile to the parking area for Lake Wood. The lake is located about 0.25 mile down a gravel road from the parking lot.

SPECIAL PICNIC SPOTS AND PLACES OF SPECIAL INTEREST

Acadia National Park is filled with interesting and lovely places to picnic and play. The following is a short list of some not-to-be-missed favorites.

Cadillac Mountain Summit. A trip to Acadia National Park would not be complete without driving to the summit of the park's highest peak, Cadillac Mountain (1,530 feet), the highest point of land along the entire Atlantic coast. Arrive before sunrise and be among the first in North America to experience the first rays of sunlight! Sunrise is awesome, but a visit at sunset or any other time of day is also worthwhile. A short trail (under 1 mile) with informative interpretive signs circumscribes the bare granite summit, and the views are truly unequaled. Check at the visitor center for ranger-led talks held daily at the summit. During September and October, Cadillac Mountain is also an excellent place to view the hawk migration.

To reach the summit, access the Park Loop Road at the Cadillac Mountain Entrance just off Route 233 west of Bar Harbor. Drive south about 1 mile on the Park Loop Road to the turnoff to the left for Cadillac Mountain. (The Cadillac Mountain turnoff is past the turnoff to the one-way portion of the Park Loop Road; do not head down the one-way portion of the Park Loop Road.) Turn left at the Cadillac Mountain turnoff and drive approximately 3.5 miles to the large parking area at the summit.

Seawall Picnic Area is perfect for seaside picnics and beach exploring. Picnic tables and grills by a cobble beach make dining al fresco easy and immensely attractive. Space is limited, however, so arrive early to claim a spot. Find Seawall Picnic Area directly opposite Seawall Campground at the southwestern tip of Mount Desert Island, off Route 102A.

Peregrine Falcon Viewing at the Precipice Cliff, Mount Champlain. Since 1990, peregrine falcons have been nesting on the Precipice Cliff of Champlain Mountain. Each spring and summer for the past five years, Acadia has hosted new falcon chicks. From the Precipice Trail parking area, visitors can observe young falcons displaying attack and chase behaviors. Until immature falcons are able to hunt and care for themselves, the park service closes the Precipice Trail to hikers. During this time, a ranger or volunteer naturalist is stationed at the Precipice Trail parking area with a telescope for close-up views of the falcons, from 9:00 A.M. to noon daily, weather permitting.

Find the Precipice Trail parking area by driving the one-way Park Loop Road about 2 miles south of the Sieur De Monts entrance to the Precipice parking lot on the right (west) side of the road. To return to Bar Harbor after departing the parking area, drive 1.1 miles south on the Park Loop Road and take a left at the Schooner Head Overlook sign. (Do not drive through the park entrance station.) Turn left again onto Schooner Head Road, which leads back to Bar Harbor and Route 3.

Schoodic Peninsula requires a fairly long drive from Mount Desert Island, but the scenery, isolation, and dramatic beauty of the peninsula are worth pursuing. Touring and picnicking families will find a wealth of oceanside picnic areas and enchanting scenic overlooks. Arrive in the early morning for the best chance of seeing deer or moose. See trips 19, Little Moose Island, and 20, Anvil Trail, for driving directions.

The Indian Point–Blagen Preserve, owned by The Nature Conservancy, on Mount Desert Island provides families with a wonderful opportunity to observe harbor seals from scenic viewpoints along the shore. Even if seals do not make an appearance (but they usually do), this sanctuary is one of the most beautiful spots on the island. Do not forget your binoculars, and be sure to

Sketching off the bridge at Indian Point–Blagen Preserve

obey all preserve restrictions. See trip 18, Indian Point Woods and Shore Trail, for driving directions.

Little Long Pond is one of Acadia National Park's scenic gems. Whether you are picnicking, hiking, or paddling its quiet waters, the pond is a beautiful retreat in all seasons. Nearby at Seal Harbor is a cobble beach and a delightful lobster shack where families can dine informally at picnic tables by the scenic harbor. There are few better places at sunset. See trip 11, Little Long Pond Loop, for driving directions.

BLUEBERRY PICKING

In August, scrumptious blueberries grace nearly every trail in Acadia. Nevertheless, if you want to pick berries in large quantities (and help your kids bake their first blueberry pie), you will want to go to a commercial picking location. On Mount Desert Island, you can reach such a field by driving south from Somesville on Route 102 about 4.5 miles to Seal Cove Road on the right. Turn right and drive west 0.6 mile until you reach Long Pond Road. Turn right and drive north about 1 mile, watching for signs advertising berry picking. Rates are reasonable and by mid-August the berries are delicious!

SECRET GARDENS

Visit in the early morning or just before dusk, and let the beauty and solitude of Mount Desert Island's gardens cast their spell.

Asticou Azalea Garden. A sand path leads visitors through meticulously designed spaces with a tranquil and elegant Japanese feel. Visit in spring or early summer to see the exuberant blooms of the abundant azaleas. In every season, sense the magic of the moss garden, step on stones across a running stream, and visit the unique Zen sand garden. Open daylight hours, from May 1 through October 31. No pets or picnicking allowed. Located off Route 198, just 0.1 mile north of the junction of Routes 3 and 198 in Northeast Harbor. Watch for a subtle sign marking the parking lot for the garden.

Thuya Garden. The best way to visit this beautiful, walled garden involves a short hike (see trip 12, Asticou Terraces, Thuya Garden, and Eliot Mountain). The garden is open daily from 7:00 A.M. to 7:00 P.M. Located on Route 3, Northeast Harbor, 0.4 mile southeast of the junction of Routes 3 and 198 (207-276-3344).

Wild Gardens of Acadia. This garden is wholly composed of native plants found on the mountains, shoreline, and forests of Acadia National Park. The plants are grouped according to their ecological niches and labeled for easy identification. Open daily, 24 hours a day. Located in Acadia National Park at Sieur de Monts, just off the Park Loop Road.

ROCK CLIMBING

For families seeking climbing instruction or guided climbs, contact Acadia Mountain Guides regarding their half- and full-day family programs (137 Cottage Street, Bar Harbor; 207-288-0342 or 288-8186). Families may also contact the Atlantic Climbing School (24 Cottage Street, Bar Harbor; 207-288-2521). For some additional experience, particularly in inclement weather, the indoor artificial-rock climbing wall at the Mount Desert Island YMCA in Bar Harbor poses challenges for novices and experts of all ages (23 Mount Desert Street, Bar Harbor; 207-288-3511).

HORSE-DRAWN CARRIAGE RIDES

Children will be enchanted by a ride in a horse-drawn carriage on one of the beautiful carriage roads within Acadia National Park. Tours may be combined with a stop at the lovely Jordan Pond House for their famous afternoon tea and popovers. There are six different tours daily ranging from 1 to 2 hours. Call Wildwood Stables for reservations (207-276-3622).

BUS AND TROLLEY TOURS OF ACADIA NATIONAL PARK

Board an old-fashioned open-air trolley or sightseeing bus and take an entertaining, narrated tour of Acadia National Park and historic Bar Harbor. Several different options are available, from 1 to 2.5 hours. Most children enjoy the 1-hour trolley ride, and may even get to ring the trolley bell! Call Acadia and Island Tours for reservations on Oli's Trolley (62 Maine Street, Bar Harbor; 207-288-9899) or Acadia National Park Tours (53 Main Street, Bar Harbor; 207-288-3327).

RAINY-DAY FAMILY RECREATION

In inclement weather, families can take cover in a variety of interesting places. Do not, however, be afraid of braving the outdoors

Thuya Garden

in a little fog and mist. With the proper precautions and foul-weather gear, foggy days can be some of Acadia's finest. For truly cold, soggy days, consult the Museums section earlier in this chapter or try the following child pleasers.

Jackson Laboratory is the world's leading mammalian research institute. A free film and lecture are offered on selected days of the week. Located on Route 3 in Bar Harbor (207-288-3371).

Mount Desert Island Biological Laboratory offers a free visitor's tour, including a video and examination of the fish specimens used in its research. Conducted Wednesdays at 1:30 P.M. throughout the summer. Located at Salisbury Cove, just off Route 3, about 5 miles from Bar Harbor.

Oz Books. This small but wonderful bookstore on Mount Desert Island offers an extraordinary children's collection. Oz Books also hosts many signings and special events throughout the summer. Located on Main Street, Southwest Harbor (207-244-9077).

Port in a Storm Bookstore has cozy, cat-filled reading areas. Located on Main Street, Route 102, Somesville (207-244-4114).

Criterion Theater. This charming theater of authentic art deco design is listed on the National Register of Historic Places. If it is raining in Bar Harbor at noon, the Criterion will run a matinee at 2:00 P.M. Located on Cottage Street in downtown Bar Harbor (207-288-3441).

Nancy Neal Typecraft Printing Museum and Memorabilia Shop. This unique museum/store has drawers upon

The Beehive: a fun and challenging climb

drawers of antique wood type. The letters can be used for printing or as decorative objects in an endless variety of craft projects. Creativity will flow in this little shop with the help of the gracious hosts who are eager to share the history of their collection. Open "by chance or appointment." Located on Steamboat Wharf Road in Bernard, 4 miles beyond Southwest Harbor (207-244-5192).

Jordan Pond House. Rainy afternoons are a perfect time to indulge in an old Acadia tradition: tea and popovers at the Jordan Pond House. Scenically situated at the south end of Jordan Pond, surrounded by forest and mountains, the restaurant specializes in deliciously hot, fresh popovers and homemade ice cream. If the skies clear, enjoy a walk on the adjacent self-guided Jordan Pond Nature Trail, the Jordan Pond Shore Trail, or the carriage road that runs by the pond. Open 11:30 A.M. to 8:00 P.M. Tea on the lawn, weather permitting, is served from 2:30 P.M. to 5:30 P.M. Reservations are recommended (207-276-3316). For driving directions, see trip 8, Penobscot and Sargent Mountains.

CHAPTER

2

Hiking Eastern Acadia National Park

The shape of Mount Desert Island is often compared to the claws of a lobster, with a larger claw to the east, a slightly smaller claw to the west, and Somes Sound between the two. The eastern "claw" is the busier side, where the bustling town of Bar Harbor and the elegant hamlet of Northeast Harbor are located. The eastern side also boasts the park's popular carriage roads, its most classically scenic ponds, most visited beach, and most frequented mountain peaks, including Mount Desert's highest summit, Cadillac Mountain. The wonderfully picturesque Park Loop Road also runs through the eastern side of Acadia National Park. In fact, the eastern lobe of Mount Desert Island offers so many excellent trails and scenic attractions that many visitors never leave that half of the island!

Families hiking on the eastern side of Acadia National Park can choose from a rich array of fun and challenging hikes. The region's offerings range from the easiest family hikes (trips 2, Ocean Trail, 6, Jesup Trail/Hemlock Road Loop, 11, Little Long Pond Loop, and 12, Asticou Terraces, Thuya Garden, and Eliot Mountain) to the most challenging climbs (trips 3, The Beehive Loop, 8, Penobscot and Sargent Mountains, and 10, South Bubble and Bubble Rock) and the longest trek (trip 5, South Ridge of Cadillac Mountain). In between are some incredibly scenic hikes where a moderate amount of effort brings rich rewards (trips 1,

Great Head Trail, 4, Gorham Mountain and the Bowl Loop, 7, Hunters Beach, and 9, Pemetic Mountain).

Although eastern Acadia is admittedly more crowded than other portions of Acadia National Park, it is distinguished by the bare granite summits of its many mountains. Consequently, almost all of the featured trails in this region provide spectacular panoramic vistas of surrounding peaks, ponds, and sea. Peak baggers in search of postcard-pretty views will be thrilled by the summit climbs on the park's eastern side.

In addition to superlative vistas, the eastern side of Acadia National Park offers Blackwoods Campground. The region also provides the island's finest gardens, including Thuya, Asticou, and Wild Gardens of Acadia at Sieur de Monts. Also at Sieur de Monts, visitors find the Nature Center and Abbe Museum of Stone Age Antiquities. Finally, while touring the eastern side, do not miss the renowned seaside attractions at Sand Beach, Great Head, Thunder Hole, and Otter Cliffs as well as tide pooling at Otter Point. Note also that many of the National Park Service's island tours leave from the dock at Northeast Harbor. There are indeed a wealth of attractions on the island's busy eastern side!

1

Great Head Trail

TYPE: Hiking Trail
DIFFICULTY: Moderate
DISTANCE: 1.5-mile loop
USAGE: High
STARTING ELEVATION: Sea level
HIGH POINT: 145 feet
SEASON: Spring, summer, fall

Climb the cliffs above Sand Beach for sweeping ocean views and exhilarating sea breezes. Take a picnic and enjoy a peaceful lunch far from the madding crowd at Sand Beach. Children will enjoy the easy rock scrambling, and parents will appreciate the drama

View of Great Head from Gorham Mountain summit

of hiking the highest point along Mount Desert's rocky coastline. This hike offers huge scenic rewards for very little effort.

Drive the Park Loop Road to Sand Beach (located 0.3 mile past the park entrance station) and park in Sand Beach's lower parking lot. Descend stairs to the beach, then walk across the beach to its eastern end. At high tide, it may be necessary to cross a shallow channel at the end of the beach to reach the Great Head peninsula. Beyond the channel, find a cedar post identifying the Great Head Trail.

Before beginning the trail, scoop up a handful of Sand Beach's colorful sand. Most sand consists of pulverized rock, but this sand is composed primarily of shell fragments and other parts of marine animals. Note the specks of green from sea urchins and purple-gray of mussel shells.

At the cedar post, hike up granite stairs to a grassy intersection. Bear right. Switchback up the ledge, following blue blazes. After 0.1 mile, arrive at another trail junction and again bear right. Continue climbing, keeping sight of blazes and cairns.

With each step or scramble, the views improve. Catch your breath at an impressive overlook of Sand Beach. Above the beach to the northwest is the hump of pink granite called the Beehive.

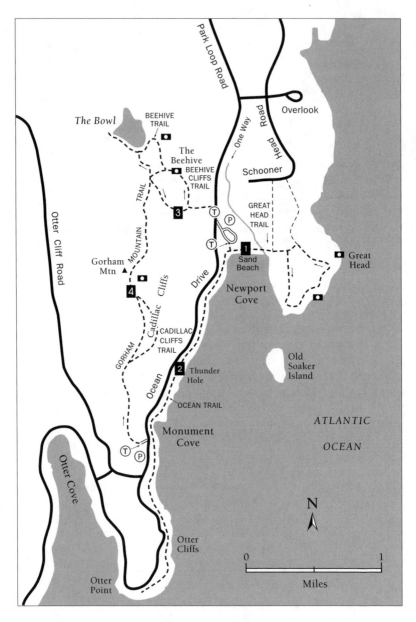

On most days, a line of antlike hikers scales its eastern cliffs. Looming north of the Beehive is Champlain Mountain whose precipitous eastern face is seasonally closed to hiking to protect its nesting peregrine falcons. Just south, find the gentle summit of Gorham Mountain. Along the shoreline, south of Sand Beach, is Thunder Hole.

Follow the trail as it heads to the southern tip of Great Head peninsula. Wide and wonderful ocean views include Otter Cliffs and the Cranberry Islands to the south. On the bogs of Little and Great Cranberry Islands, farmers once harvested the tart red fruit. Early American sailors ate the vitamin C–rich cranberries to avoid scurvy, the scourge of the sea. While it is well known that English sailors were called limeys for eating limes, it is a lesser-known fact that American seamen were called "crannies." Cranberries are no longer grown on the islands, for the bogs were drained to control mosquitoes. Today, the cranberries are lost, but the bugs remain. The little island closest to Great Head is Old Soaker Island.

Everywhere atop the water bob colorful lobster buoys, marking the location of lobster traps. Each fisherman recognizes his buoys by their color pattern. Working lobstermen set between 300 and 1,400 traps. Overfishing is avoided by the strict regulation of the size of the lobsters that can be legally harvested. By law, lobstermen must always return reproducing females to the sea. Before releasing a pregnant female, the lobsterman notches her tail so that the next time she is caught, she is immediately recognized and set free.

Given our love of lobster and the high prices it demands, it is hard to believe that Americans once considered this crustacean barely edible. In the early 1800s people ate lobster only if they were very poor. In fact, families would hide the shells so that neighbors would not know they had reached such desperate straits. Furthermore, indentured servants demanded that their contracts specify that they be served lobster only a few times a week. It was not until 1850 that lobster began to be sold in Boston, and in those days, the asking price was only three cents a lobster!

The trail turns north to travel up the eastern side of the peninsula. To the right of the trail is a jumble of dark rock that can be explored very carefully. This area of broken rock is called a "shatter zone" and represents a violent geologic intrusion of molten rock millions of years ago. The darkness of the rock is softened by summer flowers growing in the scant soil between the boulders.

Continue north and look to the east-facing cliffs of Great Head. A huge profile appears, with eye, nose, and hair discernible. After viewing the profile, rise to Great Head's highest point, 145 feet above sea level, reached in about 0.75 mile from the parking area. To the left are the ruins of an old teahouse built by a wealthy family. It is indeed a prime spot. From this height, water is visible in three directions. To the east across Frenchman Bay is the beautiful Schoodic Peninsula, to the north are the Porcupine Islands of Bar Harbor, and to the south is Baker Island and lighthouse. The drama of the site is timeless, as granite meets the sea in a ceaseless clash of rock and waves.

After the ruins, the trail descends into a lovely beech grove. At the next trail junction, bear left and rise again on pink granite ledges to head back toward Sand Beach. Views along this stretch are also magnificent. Follow the trail southwest to another intersection in 0.1 mile. Turn right and complete the loop by making a short descent to Sand Beach.

2

Ocean Trail

TYPE: Hiking Trail
DIFFICULTY: Easy
DISTANCE: 2 miles one way
USAGE: Very high
STARTING ELEVATION: Sea level
HIGH POINT: 110 feet
SEASON: Year-round

Feel the wind, taste the salt spray, and hear the crashing waves as you stroll this easy path along the dramatic shoreline from Sand Beach to Otter Point. For children there are numerous trailside diversions, including Thunder Hole, Monument Cove, and Otter Cliffs. The scenery is marvelous, but be forewarned that the trail runs parallel to the busy Park Loop Road and carries hundreds of sightseers daily. For a measure of solitude, hike this trail in the early morning.

Drive one-way Park Loop Road 0.3 mile past the park entrance station to Sand Beach (approximately 9 miles south of the Hulls

Cove Visitor Center at the start of Park Loop Road). Park in the upper Sand Beach parking lot.

The mostly level Ocean Trail begins at the southern end of the parking area. The ocean is just to your left, and frequent spur trails lead to ledges ripe for exploring and picnicking. Stroll south along the smooth path a short 0.6 mile to Thunder Hole, where waves rush into a narrow rock tunnel and cause a pocket of air to explode with a thunderous boom. For the most dramatic effect, visit on a windy day and arrive 2 hours before or after high tide. For the best vantage point, descend a flight of stairs to reach an observation area at the edge of the chasm.

After visiting Thunder Hole, return to the main trail and continue south. Watch for poison ivy growing on the trail's margins. More friendly species along the trail include shade-giving white spruce, staghorn sumac (feel its fuzzy stalks, like a deer's antlers in velvet), and, at your feet, mountain cranberry and Canada dogwood, both sporting small red berries in late summer. Early settlers ate both berries, but not without a considerable amount of sweetener!

Just past Thunder Hole, arrive at Monument Cove, a small beach strewn with countless egg-shaped rocks, worn perfectly smooth by the rolling waves. In the early days of this country, these smooth stones, called cobbles, paved the streets of eastern cities as far south as Philadelphia. A 30-foot-high sea stack (a tower of rock eroded by waves) gives the cove its name. When the waves are high, listen for the tumbling of the rocks at the water's edge. But please do not take souvenir specimens. It is against park rules.

Pass another small bay, then walk though more spruce and fir to reach Otter Cliffs, 1.5 miles from the trailhead. Several spur trails on your left lead to the cliff's edge. Use extreme caution when approaching, for there are no guardrails. Inch up to the edge, nevertheless, for you will want to catch the drama of this 110-foot drop, where rock climbers often dangle above the crashing waves.

Otter Cliffs hold a special significance in the history of Mount Desert Island. Before the discovery of the island by Europeans, the Penobscot Indians camped annually just south at Otter Creek. In 1604, French explorer Samuel Champlain sailed close by Otter Cliffs, drawn to the point by the smoke of a Penobscot encampment. Champlain was on a mission to find Norumbega, a fictional

View north from the Ocean Trail

city rumored to have walls of gold. In his quest, however, he sailed too close to the cliffs and hit a rock ledge, today marked by a clanging bell buoy just offshore. Forced to sail into Otter Cove to repair his ship, Champlain met friendly Indians who guided him around the island. Consequently he was able to create a fairly accurate map and confirm that the great golden city did not exist. On this journey, Champlain wrote that the island consisted of seven or eight mountains whose summits were mostly rock. "I named it l'Isle des Monts-deserts" (the island of bare mountains), he wrote in his diary. Almost 400 years hence, the name remains.

Continue on the main trail 0.3 mile to reach Otter Point. Here families can scamper down to the shore to picnic, tide pool, or simply gaze at the scenery. When the tide is low, the tide pooling here is excellent. Even at high tide, there is always something to watch: lobstermen checking their traps, dark cormorants diving for fish, black and white eider ducks bobbing atop the swells.

To return to the parking lot, retrace your steps along the Ocean Trail.

―――――――――――――――――――――― 3 ――――――――――――――――――――――

The Beehive Loop

TYPE: Hiking trail
DIFFICULTY: Strenuous
DISTANCE: 1.5-mile loop
USAGE: High
STARTING ELEVATION: Sea level
HIGH POINT: 542 feet
SEASON: Spring, summer, fall

For spectacular, cliff-hanging views (literally!), this is the hike to try. It is *not* for the fainthearted or for those even mildly afraid of heights. With the help of steel rungs, hikers scale the sheer granite cliffs of a beehive-shaped mountain. For those up to the challenge, the experience is heavenly, especially on a clear, windless day. It is a wonderful introduction to rock climbing, but not recommended for children under 10.

A note for parents: Although strong, intrepid youngsters will love the climb, they must be watched at all times. If parents are not comfortable with heights, they should avoid this hike.

Drive to the parking area for Sand Beach as described in trip 2, Ocean Trail. Park in Sand Beach's upper lot, then cross the Park Loop Road to find the trailhead, about 100 feet north (right) of the parking lot.

Begin on stairlike rocks and climb gently through a lovely stand of birch. Soon the footing turns to ledge. Follow blue blazes and cairns up the rock. At 0.2 mile from the trailhead, arrive at a fork marked by a large cairn. Look up to the hive-shaped mountain rising directly to the west. This is an excellent vantage point from which to watch climbers ascending the mountain's sheer cliffs. Stay right for the Beehive Cliffs Trail. The trail to the left takes hikers gradually up the back side of the Beehive. If members of your party want to skip the cliff-hanging part of this trail, they can take this trail to the left and meet climbers at the top.

Beehive Climbers, stay right. The trail wastes no time beginning its steep ascent. Climb stairs that hug the side of the cliff and pass over a small bridge of steel bars. Immediately gain great

Climbing the Beehive

views of Sand Beach and Great Head. Climbers are occasionally buffered by sturdy little pitch pines growing on the cliffs. At your feet, hardy mountain cranberries also thrive.

Continue to climb carefully, using iron rungs for foot- and handholds. Ladders take hikers straight up the cliff at the steepest parts. Watch all youngsters with extreme vigilance. The dropoffs are sheer and ever-present.

The view expands with the ascent. To the northeast, view Frenchman Bay and the Porcupine Islands; directly north are the famous cliffs of Champlain Mountain and visible to the northwest looms Cadillac Mountain. Climb carefully, allowing descending climbers time and room to negotiate down the same path.

Finally the ledge levels and climbers reach the top of the Beehive, about 0.3 mile from the trailhead. If you brought refreshments, there is room on the summit to rest and celebrate your ascent. In any event, climbers will want to drink in the fabulous views. To continue the loop, follow the trail through gray birches. Stay on the main trail as several spur trails lead to scenic overlooks. Pass by a large cairn, then descend into trees. Arrive at a post marking a trail junction about 0.1 mile from the summit. Bear left to loop back to the parking area. The trail straight ahead goes to the Bowl (trip 4, Gorham Mountain and the Bowl Loop).

Descend steeply down a rocky trail surrounded by slender white birch. The trail dips into a ravine, then rises to a trail junction about 0.2 mile from the summit. At the junction, turn left to descend toward the Park Loop Road.

In 0.1 mile, arrive at another junction. Stay left (straight) and continue to descend through deciduous forest. After 0.3 mile, emerge onto ledge and on the left meet the trail ascending the Beehive. Stay right and keep descending, retracing your steps to the Sand Beach parking area.

4

Gorham Mountain and the Bowl Loop

TYPE: Hiking trail
DIFFICULTY: Moderate
DISTANCE: 4.5 miles round trip
USAGE: High
STARTING ELEVATION: Sea level
HIGH POINT: 525 feet
SEASON: Spring, summer, fall

This is one of the finest family trails in the park, especially on a warm summer day. The trail offers sweeping vistas, superb pond swimming, beaver lodges, ancient sea caves, and myriad options to please hikers of all ages and abilities. Families with older children may want to combine this loop with the titillating climb up the steep eastern face of the Beehive (trip 3, The Beehive Loop). In any event, do not forget picnic lunches, bathing suits, binoculars, and plenty of liquids.

Drive to Gorham Mountain trailhead parking lot, located 1 mile south of Sand Beach on the right side of the Park Loop Road. Park in the lot and find the trailhead in the woods on the southwest side of the lot.

The trail heads first through a stand of pitch pines. All pitch pines have needles in bundles of three. Children can remember its name by recalling an umpire's shout after a *pitch*: "Strrrrrike *three*, you're out!" Pitch pines love dry, rocky ledges. They are often the only trees on exposed coastal ridges and mountain summits, for they can survive the onslaught of wind and salt. Watch out; the cones of pitch pine have sharp thorns at the tips of their scales.

Follow cairns and climb gently to a fork 0.2 mile from the trailhead. Be alert for the fork, for it is easy to miss. From this fork, both trails lead to the summit and reach it in 0.7 mile. The trail to the left climbs quickly to great views and travels pleasantly atop an open ridge. The trail to the right runs along the shady base of Cadillac Cliffs for 0.5 mile before meeting up with the scenic Gorham Mountain Trail. Although the Cadillac Cliffs Trail is less beautiful, it is a more challenging and exciting route for youngsters.

Those taking the view-filled Gorham Mountain Trail, simply bear left and follow the cairns north over the granite to the next trail junction. Adventurous hikers turn right. Scramble over a jumble of rocks and broken ledges, following cairns and blazes. The path rises gently, hugging massive Cadillac Cliffs on the left. A broken ledge that fell over the trail creates a 10-foot-long "tunnel" through which the entire family can pass. Just beyond, to the left of the trail, ask the children to find a "Flintstone" home. Youngsters will be delighted to find ancient sea caves in the side of the cliff that could pass (with a little imagination) as shallow cliff dwellings.

Long ago these caves stood under the ocean and were probably home not to Fred and Wilma, but to large and less friendly sea creatures. Pause for a moment and ask the children what they

"Fishing" for minnows at the Bowl

hear. Although out of view, crashing waves and often Thunder
Hole itself are audible. Listen for the bell buoy ringing as it rides
the waves just off Otter Point. After the trail passes the last cave,
cross over a crevice on a wooden bridge and then climb steeply on
stone stairs to a trail junction with the upper trail.

At the junction, to continue up the mountain, those who as-
cended the stairs turn right and hikers who took the upper trail
stay left. From this intersection, all hikers climb on open granite
ledges that afford spectacular views for the remaining 0.4 mile to
the summit. Be forewarned: a false summit disappoints children
who believe they have made it to the top. The true summit is
marked by a large cairn and wooden sign.

Reach the summit at about 0.9 mile from the trailhead. The
views are truly superb—a 200-degree water view. To the north and
east is Frenchman Bay, dotted with the Porcupine Islands. Directly east and over 500 feet below are Sand Beach and Great Head
peninsula. To the south lies Otter Point and, across Eastern Way,
the Cranberry Islands. Directly north is the rocky face of the Beehive (525 feet). Pull out your map to identify the many landmarks
you will see in this glorious panoramic view, one of the prettiest
in the park.

After resting at the summit and sampling blueberries from the bushes that adorn its ledges, descend to the Bowl for a refreshing swim. To reach the Bowl, continue north, following cairns for about 0.4 mile. At 1.3 miles from the trailhead, the trail descends more steeply, plunging into shady woods. At 1.5 miles from the trailhead (0.6 mile from the summit), meet a trail junction. The trail to the right descends to the Park Loop Road. Take the trail to the left and climb moderately northwest for nearly 0.2 mile, and then drop suddenly to the Bowl.

The Bowl is a fabulous place for picnicking and swimming. Large, flat rocks on the lake's east shore provide the best spots for laying out lunch and launching into the water. The eight-acre lake warms up nicely by midsummer. Countless minnows amuse youngsters who could spend hours trying to catch them, while the lake's brook trout attract more serious fishermen. For explorers, a trail travels around the south end of the lake. Beaver lodges are visible on the lake's northwestern end. You probably will not see beaver during the day, but challenge the kids to find signs of beaver activity. Look for gnawed-off tree stumps (which look like crudely sharpened pencils). Hint: there are fresh stumps along the trail where you entered the Bowl.

Do not leave the Bowl without hiking about 0.1 mile northeast for more tremendous panoramic views. First follow the trail north along the southeastern shore. The trail turns sharply right (east) and climbs steeply over a ledge. Soon it arrives on open baldface with great views of Champlain Mountain to the north, Gorham Mountain to the south, and the Atlantic to the southeast.

To continue the loop, return to the Bowl and exit the way you entered, at the lake's south end. Hike 0.2 mile back to the trail junction. This time, continue southeast on the trail that descends to the Park Loop Road in 0.6 mile. The rocky trail passes through a young but dense birch forest that is spectacular in the fall. The trail to the Beehive enters on the left, but stay right to continue descending east past a boulderfield. Take a moment at the trail junction, however, to watch the intrepid climbers on Beehive's steep eastern face (see trip 3, The Beehive Loop).

Just 0.2 mile past the boulderfield, reach the Park Loop Road. Carefully cross the road, and walk south (right) just 100 yards to the entrance to the parking lot for Sand Beach. Just south of the lot entrance, on the east side of the Park Loop Road, the Ocean

Trail runs along the coastline, closely paralleling the road. To return to your car, follow the level Ocean Trail for 1 mile to the Gorham Mountain trailhead parking lot on the west side of the road. Ocean views and cool winds make this a pleasant stroll (see trip 2, Ocean Trail).

5

South Ridge of Cadillac Mountain

TYPE: Hiking trail
DIFFICULTY: Strenuous
DISTANCE: 3.7 miles one way
USAGE: Moderate
STARTING ELEVATION: 100 feet
HIGH POINT: 1,530 feet
SEASON: Spring, summer, fall

The South Ridge Trail is Cadillac Mountain's most scenic ascent. After the first wooded mile, the trail rises along the granite spine of Mount Desert Island's tallest mountain, affording nonstop, sweeping, and spectacular views. This trail is highly recommended for tenacious hikers who appreciate wide-open spaces and breathtaking panoramas. Bring water, sunscreen, and a jacket to ward off cold summit winds.

From Bar Harbor, drive south on Route 3 about 5 miles to find the trailhead about 50 yards west of the Blackwoods Campground entrance. A cedar post marks the Cadillac Mountain South Ridge trailhead. Park along the road.

The first mile climbs through a dark, mixed forest. Watch out for roots studding the path. Gradually the forest begins to open, and hikers must follow cairns across rock outcrops. At approximately 1 mile from the trailhead, arrive at a junction with the short spur trail to Eagles Crag. This 0.1-mile detour to the right takes hikers to a rocky promontory overlooking the Otter Creek area. Take this brief detour. The Eagles Crag spur trail loops north to meet the main trail about 0.1 mile further up the trail.

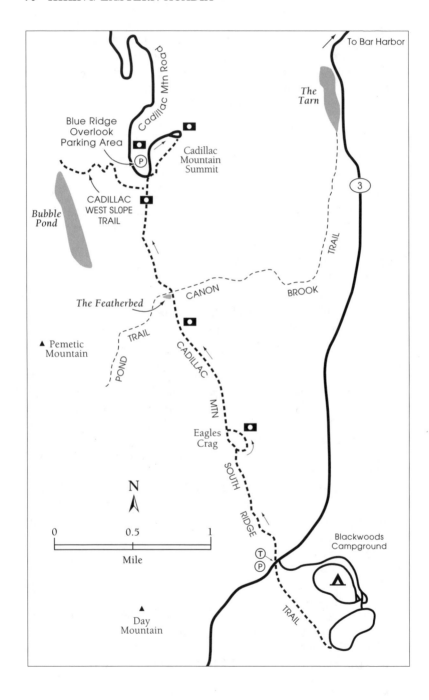

To Bar Harbor

Cadillac Mtn Road

The Tarn

Blue Ridge Overlook Parking Area

(P)

Cadillac Mountain Summit

CADILLAC WEST SLOPE TRAIL

Bubble Pond

3

BROOK

TRAIL

The Featherbed

CANON

TRAIL

▲ Pemetic Mountain

POND

CADILLAC

MTN

Eagles Crag

SOUTH

RIDGE

N
⋀

0   0.5   1

Mile

(T)
(P)

Blackwoods Campground

⛺

TRAIL

▲ Day Mountain

Continuing on the South Ridge Trail, the views steadily improve as the forest drops away. The trail climbs fairly gently over sloping ledge with unobstructed panoramic views. Cadillac Mountain's south ridge drops precipitously on its west and east sides into broad valleys. To the east are marvelous views of the Bowl, a little round lake beneath a small rocky hump called the Beehive. Champlain Mountain dominates the view to the northeast.

Climb next to a rocky knoll. After taking in the views, descend to the Featherbed, a pretty little glacial cirque rimmed by pitch pines and gray birch. The rush-filled Featherbed (hence its name) is a lovely pond in midsummer, but may be just a pleasant marsh by August. This is a good spot to rest, as wooden benches are set conveniently on the edge of the windblown rushes.

Near the pond, trails descend steeply to the left and right. Continue straight on the South Ridge Trail. Just past the Featherbed, the trail rises steeply, but briefly, through a grove of gray birch to more magnificent views. Hikers now have just 1 mile remaining to the summit, and what a miracle mile it is! Views are stupendous in all directions. Bring your park map to locate the park's myriad peaks, lakes, bays, islands, and peninsulas. Closest to the west is Pemetic Mountain (trip 9), and to the northeast is Dorr Mountain. This expansive ledge is an excellent place for a picnic, and it is likely to be less crowded and breezy than the summit.

After climbing gently another 0.5 mile, reach the intersection with the West Slope Trail descending steeply to the left. Continue straight (north), following cairns. Low huckleberry and blueberry bushes adorn the granite. About 0.1 mile from the trail junction, reach Cadillac Mountain Road. The South Ridge Trail continues climbing northeast just south of the road. In the 0.3-mile climb remaining to the summit, the trail loses views and ascends sometimes steeply through the pines. Just before reaching the summit, hikers meet a gravel fireroad that descends to the back of the Cadillac Mountain Gift Shop and large parking lot.

A good alternative to this rough and less than scenic final leg is to turn right (uphill) on the Cadillac Mountain Road (toward the Blue Ridge Overlook parking area) and hike the road to the summit. Of course, this alternative is attractive only if traffic is light. The views and footing are better, and the summit can be easily reached in less than 10 minutes.

Rock cairns help hikers find their way.

To return to the trailhead, regain the South Ridge Trail behind the gift shop or descend on the road. Road hikers should pass the Blue Ridge Overlook parking area and look immediately to the left to find the South Ridge Trail. The trip down offers spectacular views of the Cranberry Islands directly to the south and the many islands of Frenchman Bay, as well as the peaks and valleys of most of Mount Desert Island.

6

Jesup Trail/Hemlock Road Loop

> TYPE: Hiking trail
> DIFFICULTY: Easy
> DISTANCE: 1.4 miles round trip
> USAGE: Moderate
> STARTING ELEVATION: 80 feet
> HIGH POINT: 80 feet
> SEASON: Midsummer to fall

This wonderful, effortless walk through forest and meadow is absolutely superb for families. Children love the wooden boardwalk that courses through the most beautiful birch forest on the island. For early risers, bird-watching is excellent in Great Meadow, a freshwater marsh crossed by the path. Although the trail is exquisite in late summer and divine in autumn, avoid it in early summer when biting insects thrive in the meadow.

From Route 3 in downtown Bar Harbor, drive south on Route 3 approximately 2.5 miles and pass over the Park Loop Road. Immediately after the overpass, take the next right, at the Sieur de Monts entrance, and turn left into the large parking lot. Alternately, drive the Park Loop Road from the Hulls Cove Visitor Center about 5.8 miles to the large parking lot for Sieur de Monts Spring, the Nature Center, Wild Gardens of Acadia, and the Abbe Museum. Find the Jesup trailhead at the north end of the lot (farthest from the Nature Center). The hike begins on the gravel road behind the closed gate.

Hike briefly west on the gravel road to the intersection with the Jesup Trail. Turn right on the path and enter a beautiful forest of white birch and maple. Tall, graceful trees flank the narrow trail, bordered by a lush undergrowth of ferns and grass. A two-board, bouncy boardwalk over the boggy ground encourages children to skip like elves through the lovely, green forest.

From all directions within the forest, the black "eyes" of the birch (triangular branch scars) watch intently. White birch is arguably the most beautiful tree in Acadia. It is easily identified by its smooth, bright white bark and black horizontal slits or lenticels. Native Americans used the bark for building canoes and covering tepees, because an oil within the bark makes it waterproof. Look also for the yellow birch, whose bark is a silvery bronze that peels in thin, papery curls. Yellow birches love moist soil and can grow quite large here. Their twigs, when peeled, smell of mint, and Native Americans used them as toothpicks! In autumn, birch leaves turn a fiery yellow. Add the scarlet leaves of the red maple, and this forest is quite a special spot in early October.

This is also a lively stretch of trail. Watch for the harmless eastern garter snake, which is 1 to 2 feet long with three distinct stripes (yellow, green, or brown) running lengthwise from head to tail. Next, take a moment to stop and listen. Chipmunks are plentiful and are especially active between 9:00 A.M. and 1:00 P.M. Deer also frequent this area, particularly at dawn and dusk. In addition, a wide variety of birds inhabits this forest and the adjacent meadow. In the birch forest, look on the trunks of snags for downy

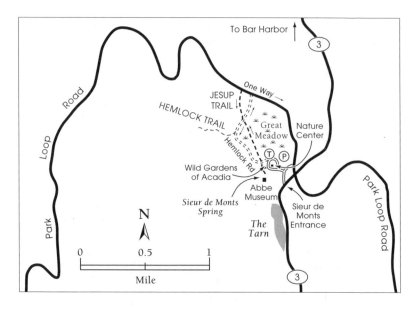

and pileated woodpeckers and everywhere for acrobatic black-capped chickadees.

Continue to the end of the bog walk and emerge from the birch-maple forest. At a fork in the trail 0.5 mile from the trailhead, stay right. The trail soon forks again, with a narrow trail on the left and a wider, more established trail on the right. In wet seasons, stay right. Both trails lead north, running parallel through Great Meadow to the Park Loop Road, so hikers can take either path.

Great Meadow, a freshwater marsh, extends left and right of the trail. Moisture-tolerant grasses, sedges, and flowers thrive here. Flanking the trail, young gray birches offer dappled shade. Children can easily distinguish gray birch by its leaves. Note how the leaf is triangular and resembles the head of an elephant. Since an elephant is gray, voilà, it is a gray birch!

The flanks of surrounding mountains are visible from the meadow and in autumn display a patchwork of russet, red, and gold. Continue north toward the Park Loop Road. Just before arriving at the road, reach a grove of quaking aspens, easily identified by their fluttering silver green leaves. Pause here and take a deep breath. Waist-high by the trail grow fragrant bushes of sweet fern. Its leaves are 3 to 6 inches long and lobed on all sides. Rub them gently between your hands, then smell the fragrance from your palms. For centuries, their sweet scent has enhanced soaps and candles. In colonial times, the added scent was essential since foul-smelling animal fats were used to make most candles and soaps.

Follow the trail to the road, turn left, and walk about 100 yards down the Park Loop Road to a cedar post marking the Jesup Trail. Turn left on the path and reenter the aspen grove. Head back through Great Meadow with the aid of boards and bridges. In the center of the meadow, pause and listen for the rustling of countless mice, voles, and moles that tunnel unseen beneath the tall grass. Usually visible are luminescent blue dragonflies.

Arrive at a fork and keep right. First skirt the edge of the meadow, then enter a dark forest, vastly different from the birch-maple forest encountered earlier. You have entered an old-growth hemlock forest, filled with centuries-old hemlock, spruce, and cedar trees. At the next trail intersection, stay straight on this wide trail called the Hemlock Road.

The massive trunks of the old hemlocks are awesome. Recognize hemlock by its delicate, silvery foliage and tiny, perfectly formed cones that grow from the ends of the branches. The short needles grow not in neat rows, but in a whorl around the twigs. Much less light penetrates the hemlock forest and, consequently, there is little groundcover. As you continue through the forest, beech trees begin to replace the evergreens.

To return to the parking lot, follow the trail as it curves southeast. In 0.3 mile from the Hemlock Road intersection, the trail brings you to the closed gate where the hike began. Before returning to the lot, however, families may want to visit the other sights at Sieur de Monts, including the Wild Gardens of Acadia, the Nature Center, and the Abbe Museum of Stone Age Antiquities (see chapter 1, Acadia National Park: A Visitor's Overview). All can be easily reached from the Jesup Trail. Simply turn right onto the Jesup Trail (just before coming to the closed gate) and walk a few minutes through the forest. To reach the Wild Gardens of Acadia, turn left and cross a small wooden bridge over a stream. The garden is on your left, the Nature Center to your right, and the Abbe Museum just down the paved path from the Nature Center. All are well worth a visit.

7

Hunters Beach

TYPE: Hiking trail
DIFFICULTY: Easy
DISTANCE: 0.5 mile one way
USAGE: Low
STARTING ELEVATION: 120 feet
LOW POINT: Sea level
SEASON: Year-round

Escape the crowds and descend to a beautiful cobble beach via a short and scenic trail. Although there is no sand at Hunters Beach, children will find a treasure trove of multicolored dinosaur-egg–like rocks and smooth, climbable ledges. Hunters Beach is perfect for picnicking and tide pooling, and a trail through the headlands above the beach is great for young explorers. Best of all, this beach offers seclusion and untouched coastal beauty.

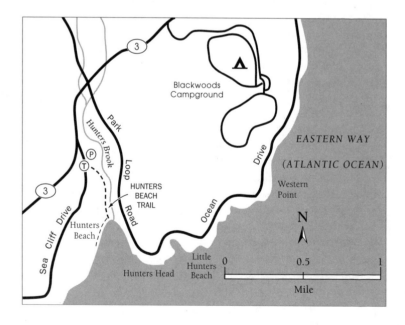

From Bar Harbor, drive south on Route 3 approximately 5.8 miles, then turn left on Sea Cliff Drive (which may not be marked). Sea Cliff Drive is located approximately 0.8 mile past the well-marked Blackwoods Campground entrance. Drive 0.2 mile further on Sea Cliff Drive to a small parking turnout on the left. Approaching on Route 3 from the west, find Sea Cliff Drive 1.3 miles west of Route 3's intersection with Jordan Pond Road. Park and find the trail marked by a cedar post.

Begin on a wide and level path through a shady forest of fir and spruce. The groundcover of moss and sarsasparilla creates a dark lushness. The path drops to cross a picturesque wooden bridge. A short section of rough trail follows, and hikers must be careful not to trip on the tangle of roots. To the left, Hunters Brook tumbles

A young naturalist enjoys the fungi.

down big boulders, its merry gurgling drowning out the last noises of civilization.

Descend to an easy crossing of an inlet via stepping stones, then walk through the last of the forest to emerge dramatically at Hunters Beach 0.5 mile from the trailhead. Countless cobbles cover the beach, worn flawlessly smooth by the tumbling waves. At low tide, find tide pools at either end of the cove. Fortune seekers can investigate the assorted driftwood and castaway treasures flung by the waves above the rack line. Those seeking shade can retreat to the spruces lining the rear of the cove. Behind the spruces, find a narrow path that rises and travels south to explore the steep cliffs that protect the cove. This is a short, fun trail to hike, but explorers should watch their footing on this narrow path, for there are sheer drop-offs.

To return, retrace your steps back to the trailhead.

8

Penobscot and Sargent Mountains

> TYPE: Hiking trail
> DIFFICULTY: Strenuous
> DISTANCE: 2.6 miles one way
> USAGE: High
> STARTING ELEVATION: 220 feet
> HIGH POINT: 1,373 feet
> SEASON: Spring, summer, fall

For an abundance of wonderful views, trek the wide-open southern spine of two magnificent mountains, Penobscot and Sargent. En route, try a little cliff scrambling and take a dip in a scenic pond nestled between the two peaks. Be prepared to share these treasures, however, for this peak-bagging hike draws a substantial number of fans. Smaller children may find the trip a bit long, but older youngsters will enjoy the challenge.

From the intersection of Route 233 and the Park Loop Road (just west of Bar Harbor), take the Park Loop Road south about 5 miles to the Jordan Pond parking area. The parking area is located just 0.1 mile north of the Jordan Pond House on the west side of Park Loop Road. Park and find the path to the boat ramp at the lot's west end (see detail map on p. 86).

Take this path to Jordan Pond's south shore, where you will meet the Jordan Pond Shore Trail. Take a left on the shore path, pass a clearing, head briefly through trees, and then emerge at a carriage road, just before a stone bridge over Jordan Stream. Turn left onto the carriage road and walk a couple hundred feet, looking to the right for a footbridge across Jordan Stream and a cedar post indicating the Sargent and Penobscot Mountain Trails. (The footbridge is just before the next carriage road intersection at Post

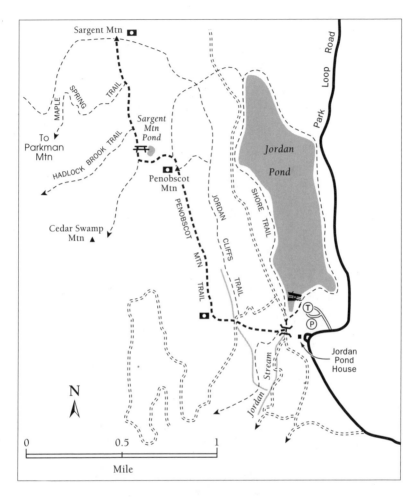

15.) Cross the footbridge and stay straight (right) at the next fork on the other side of the stream.

> **NOTE:** The Penobscot and Sargent Mountain Trails are easily reached from a trail behind the Jordan Pond House Gift Shop, which leads down to the carriage road at a point directly across from the footbridge over Jordan Stream. Due to parking congestion at the Jordan Pond House, however, the park service prefers hikers to use the larger lot north of the house.

The trail drops down a rocky slope, crosses a small brook, and arrives at another intersection, this time with the Jordan Cliffs Trail. Keep left for the Penobscot and Sargent Mountain Trails.

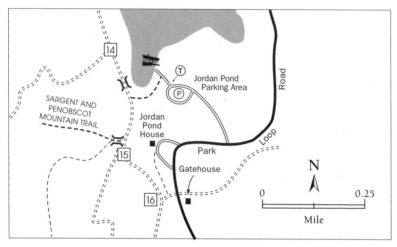

Follow the path to stone steps leading to another carriage road. Cross the road and pick up the trail on the opposite side. Here the real work begins as the trail ascends the steep cliffs of Penobscot's east slope. Follow blazes up boulders with the aid of handrails and a footbridge. Watch and assist children carefully. This stretch is challenging, but it is thankfully brief (about 0.1 mile).

Once atop the cliffs, the trail ascends one more steep slope, then levels off on a wide expanse of ledge. The trail jogs to the right, then the remaining 0.9 mile to the Penobscot summit travels a treeless granite ridge providing magnificent views and easy trekking. Jordan Pond lies far below, mountains surround you, and the vast ocean and islands stretch out endlessly to the southern horizon.

Follow cairns that grow increasingly creative and architectural. The trail takes you to the west side of the ridge for views of the deep gulch between Penobscot and Cedar Swamp Mountains. Far below, a lovely carriage road runs through this tree-filled natural amphitheater (see trip 27, Amphitheater Loop).

Descend briefly, then resume your ascent, passing a small pond on the left. Arrive finally at a huge cairn marking Penobscot's 1,194-foot summit, 1.6 miles from the trailhead. This is a good turnaround point, if your family's energy is lagging. The Sargent Mountain summit is 0.9 mile further, with an elevation loss of about 150 feet, then a gain of 323 feet. To return, simply retrace your steps.

At the Penobscot summit, those who wish to continue must find the well-marked trail to Sargent Mountain (heading northwest) and descend, following cairns and blue blazes. Reach a lush grove of spruce and continue to drop steeply. At 0.1 mile from the Penobscot summit, reach an intersection with a trail heading off to the right to Jordan Pond. Continue straight ahead. Rise gently to reach a ledge, then drop again as the trail meets the south edge of Sargent Mountain Pond. This pond was formerly and more poetically known as "Lake of the Clouds." The pretty, tree-rimmed lake is spring-fed and warms up to a tolerable swimming temperature in summer. Flat rocks at its south and north ends provide good access points. To reach the northern end, follow a trail along its west shore.

Leave the pond's edge to reach Sargent's summit. From the pond, the trail swings southwest and rises quickly to the south ridge of Sargent Mountain. Arrive at a fork and turn right (north)

Approaching Penobscot Mountain summit

for the summit. As you ascend Sargent's granite spine, the stupendous, unobstructed views return in full force. Pass briefly through some hardy spruce, then regain your vistas. Meet another trail junction (the Hadlock Brook Trail) on your left, and continue straight, rising moderately. The trail levels and one more trail enters on the left (to Parkman Mountain). Again stay straight (north). In 0.2 mile, reach the huge cairn on Sargent's summit. On the whole of Mount Desert Island, Sargent Mountain is the highest peak reachable solely by trail. Only Cadillac Mountain is taller, but its summit is marred by a road, radio tower, and gift shop.

Sargent Mountain's summit is large enough to find a solitary place to spread a picnic and celebrate your family's triumphant ascent. Take the time to savor the achievement and the marvelous views that surround you. When you are ready to return, retrace your steps to the trailhead.

9

Pemetic Mountain

TYPE: Hiking trail
DIFFICULTY: Strenuous
DISTANCE: 3.2 miles round trip
USAGE: Low
STARTING ELEVATION: 330 feet
HIGH POINT: 1,248 feet
SEASON: Spring, summer, fall

This challenging route up Pemetic Mountain offers fantastic views and a chance to escape the crowds that amass on the park's more popular peaks. Despite its relative obscurity, Pemetic Mountain rates as one of the park's most lovely and enjoyable climbs. Its steep ascent up a smooth ledge provides fun challenges for young climbers. For safety, wear sturdy, lug-soled hiking boots. This is an especially wonderful hike in fall foliage season.

Drive to a small turnout on the west side of the Park Loop Road approximately 0.4 mile north of the Jordan Pond House parking lot and about 4.8 miles south of the junction of the Park

Leaping a "crevice" on Pemetic Mountain

Loop Road and Route 233 (west of Bar Harbor).

Park at the turnout, then cross the Park Loop Road to find the cedar post marking the trailhead for Pemetic Mountain (via the Pond Trail). Enter a forest of spruce and fir and cross a small stream. The shady path rises steadily to reach a trail junction at about 0.5 mile from the trailhead. The sign indicates that continuing straight heads to the Triad. Take a sharp left at this junction to begin your ascent.

After a short distance, break out of the forest to emerge on sunny, blueberry-strewn ledge. You need only climb several minutes to gain stupendous views of the Cranberry Islands and Jordan Pond. The open ledge provides wonderfully sunny spots for catching your breath and taking in the sights.

The views continue to improve as you move up the mountain. Lose the views only momentarily as you reenter spruce forest and descend slightly. When you re-emerge onto wide-open ledge, enjoy expansive views to the west of Jordan Pond, Somes Sound, and the bare granite of the park's western peaks. The sights are fantastic, framed only by wind-sculpted spruce.

Soon the trail levels a bit and arrives at a trail junction. The sign indicates that Pemetic Mountain is 0.9 mile further, although the correct distance is closer to 0.6 mile. Keep left (north) at the junction. (The trail to the right descends to the Triad.)

The remaining hike to the summit is pure heaven. Follow prominently displayed cairns and blazes. The windswept ledge

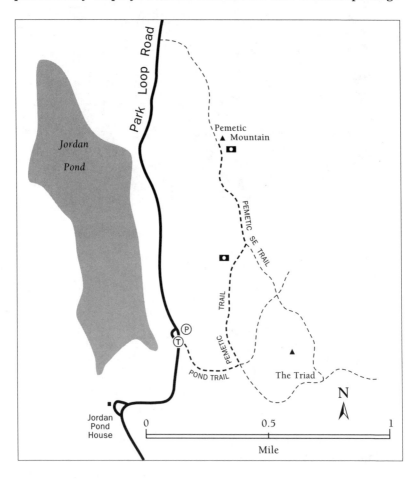

affords continuous, unobstructed views. Take out a map to identify the many peaks, valleys, ponds, and islands within your gaze.
Most prominent to the east is Cadillac Mountain, one of only three
peaks in Acadia that rise above Pemetic.

By this point, the steep sections are behind you, so the short
distance remaining to the summit is a cakewalk. A huge cairn
marks Pemetic's relatively flat summit. From the summit, take in
particularly dramatic views of the Bubbles (see Bubble Rock, precariously perched on the west side of South Bubble) and beautiful Jordan Pond more than 1,000 feet below. Good eyes will spot
antlike bicyclists cycling the carriage road on the far side of the
pond. To the northeast, take in Frenchman Bay and the Schoodic
Peninsula. Settle down for a picnic, explore the summit, and pick
some sweet blueberries in the rarefied air. Then reluctantly retrace your steps to civilization.

10

South Bubble and Bubble Rock

TYPE: Hiking trail
DIFFICULTY: Strenuous (with moderate option)
DISTANCE: 2-mile loop
USAGE: High
STARTING ELEVATION: 274 feet
HIGH POINT: 768 feet
SEASON: Spring, summer, fall

Climb to the bare pink summit of the South Bubble for outstanding views and kid-friendly attractions. This loop trail ascends one
of two granite humps rising above Jordan Pond and Eagle Lake.
Challenge youngsters to find the mysterious multi-ton, precariously set Bubble Rock and to descend a demanding rock slide. In
addition, an optional mile-long detour gives hikers the opportunity to visit beautiful Jordan Pond. The diversions and diversity
of this 2-mile loop please hikers of all ages.

From the park's visitor center at Hulls Cove, drive south on
the Park Loop Road. In 3 miles, arrive at the intersection with the

Watch out below! Bubble Rock, South Bubble

beginning of the one-way Park Loop Road. Continue straight (do not turn left onto the one-way road). Drive south on the Park Loop Road another 3 miles to the Bubble Rock parking lot on the right, 1.8 miles north of the Jordan Pond House.

The trail begins on the west side of the parking lot. Head west into a shady beech forest and immediately arrive at a trail junction. Continue straight on the ascending trail signed for South Bubble. Climb through the forest and arrive quickly at another intersection. The trail to the right leads to North Bubble. Stay left. After just 0.1 mile, arrive at yet another junction. Turn left to ascend the remaining 0.2 mile to the peak of South Bubble.

Climb first on log stairs, then break out of the forest to ascend bare granite, following blazes and cairns. Climb past scattered stands of aspen and birch to reach the summit at 768 feet. Enjoy an excellent view of Jordan Pond to the south, Eagle Lake to the north, and a wealth of surrounding peaks. Small spruce adorn the mountain top but do not obstruct the excellent views.

Let the children lead you to Bubble Rock, found just east of the summit. A glacier dropped this van-sized glacial erratic atop this mountain when it rode over this area more than 10,000 years ago. Today it appears to be balanced delicately on the side of the mountain. Youngsters may give it a shove, for it would take far more than a child to topple this boulder. The entire Mount Desert High School football team once attempted to roll it off!

There are two recommended ways to descend the South Bubble. The moderate-rated option is easiest and shortest: descend the trail you came up. The more challenging route follows a trail

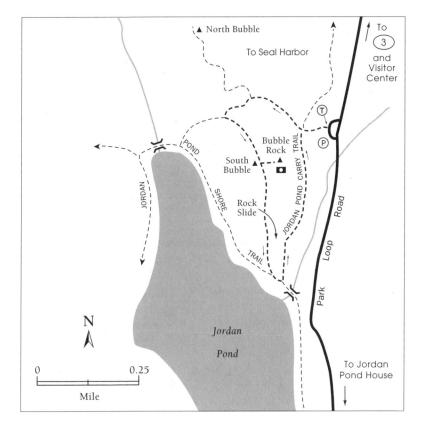

down a rock slide, where the going is steep and slippery. Tough sections require careful footwork, a slow pace, and often a five-point descent (hands, feet, and bottom). Many children enjoy the latter.

Those opting for the easier descent need only retrace their steps to their car. All others walk south along the exposed ridge of South Bubble's broad, bare summit to increasingly beautiful views of Jordan Pond, the ocean, and offshore islands. From below, North and South Bubble look like identical twin humps. Early settlers referred to the two small mountains as "the Boobies." (For the most revealing view, look north toward the two mountains from the Jordan Pond House.) Later, more conservative residents dropped the bawdy reference and adopted the less colorful name "Bubbles."

At the summit's south end, begin the 0.4-mile descent. In late summer, take a few blueberries from the mountaintop shrubs for a burst of energy. The first step is to negotiate some steep ledges. Keep a close eye on all climbers, especially children. Below the ledges, the rock slide begins. Descend slowly, for the smooth rocks can be very slick.

Finally (and thankfully!) arrive at the edge of Jordan Pond, where the descending trail meets the Jordan Pond Shore Trail and Jordan Pond Carry Trail. To return to your car, take an immediate left onto the Jordan Pond Carry Trail and follow the directions set forth in the paragraph after next. The sign indicates that the Bubble Rock parking lot is only 0.5 mile away.

Those with energy for a 1-mile scenic detour should turn right onto the Jordan Pond Shore trail and rock hop on the level trail along the pond's lovely shore. In 0.5 mile, hikers on the Jordan Pond Shore Trail arrive at the northern tip of Jordan Pond and cross a fine log bridge. A beaver lodge is visible to the right. The bridge is a good turnaround point. Return the way you came, back to the junction with the Jordan Pond Carry Trail.

From the intersection with the Jordan Pond Carry Trail, the rest of the hike is a piece of cake. Turn left onto the Carry Trail and ascend gently through shady beech forest. After 0.2 mile meet a trail that indicates a parking lot. Do *not* turn right, but continue north on the Carry Trail for another 0.2 mile in the direction of Eagle Lake. At the next intersection, turn right to reach the Bubble Rock parking lot.

—— 11 ——

Little Long Pond Loop

TYPE: Hiking trail
DIFFICULTY: Very easy (handicapped-accessible with
    assistance)
DISTANCE: 1.4-mile loop
USAGE: Moderate
STARTING ELEVATION: 8 feet
HIGH POINT: 50 feet
SEASON: Spring, summer, fall

This effortless stroll is immensely enjoyable and scenic. A grassy
trail takes hikers along the shore of Little Long Pond, perhaps the
prettiest pond on Mount Desert Island. Visit an old-fashioned,
romantic boathouse built for J. D. Rockefeller, Jr., lay a picnic in
the mowed fields above the pond, and watch while inspired children romp and cartwheel in the delightfully inviting scenery.
Beautiful in any season, but especially inspiring in fall, Little Long
Pond is an excellent choice for young families.

From Stanley Brook entrance at Seal Harbor, drive 0.7 mile
west on Route 3. Find Little Long Pond on the north side of Route

Little Long Pond

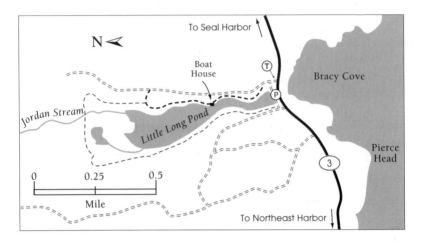

3, across from a cobble seawall at Bracy Cove. There is limited parking along the road. Little Long Pond and the surrounding land are owned by the Rockefellers, but are open for the public's quiet enjoyment. Please respect posted signs and carry out all litter.

At Little Long Pond's southeast end, access the trail via a handsome gate and begin the hike on the carriage road that travels north along the east side of the pond. Almost immediately a dirt road intersects the carriage road from the left. Stay straight, following the carriage road. About 50 yards after this junction, a wide grassy trail also intersects the road from the left. Turn left onto the grassy trail and decend gently to the water's edge.

Those with wheelchairs or strollers may want to remain on the carriage road, especially in wet seasons. The road parallels the shore path on higher, drier ground and offers excellent water views, if not intimacy with the pond itself. Bicycles are prohibited on this carriage road, so families may stroll wholly in peace.

In midsummer, the huge yellow blossoms of the water lily adorn the shallow pond. In Scandinavia, pond lilies are called *Näck* roses, after Näck, a troll who waits at the bottom of ponds, fishing for people to eat. The yellow lily is his bait, and his line, the long rootstalk. Beware all those enticed by the beauty of the flower! Apparently the park's many ducks are safe from the troll, for they frequently enjoy the nutritious seeds of the water lily.

The grassy trail continues north for about 0.5 mile until it reaches the old boathouse. Views are magnificent from its porch.

Gaze inside for a glimpse of the Rockefeller rowboat and changing rooms. One can imagine the long-skirted ladies and bow-tied, mustachioed men who once launched boats through these doors. Just north of the boathouse is a nice beach for wading.

Continue on the grassy path north of the boathouse. Look across the pond for a beaver lodge visible on the pond's west side. The path soon swings away from the water to meet the carriage road about 0.7 mile from the trailhead. Those arriving by the carriage road can use the grassy path to visit the boathouse. For variety, return to Route 3 via the carriage road. Or retrace your steps along the pond-side trail. The grassy trail is so pleasant, it is just as nice on the return. Little Long Pond is also a beautiful and tranquil spot to paddle a canoe or kayak (see trip 32, Little Long Pond).

12

Asticou Terraces, Thuya Garden, and Eliot Mountain

TYPE: Hiking trail
DIFFICULTY: Easy (Thuya Garden) to moderate (Eliot Mountain)
DISTANCE: 0.5 mile (Thuya Garden) to 1.1 miles (Eliot Mountain) one way
USAGE: High (Thuya Garden) to low (Eliot Mountain)
STARTING ELEVATION: 50 feet
HIGH POINT: 225 feet (Thuya Garden) to 456 feet (Eliot Mountain)
SEASON: July through September

This trail is a magic duo of the finest in refined, formal beauty and rugged, view-filled mountainsides, all in just over 1 mile of hiking! The trail ascends beautifully landscaped terraces to a walled formal flower garden fit for royalty, then ventures up a precipitous granite slope to the summit of little-visited Eliot Mountain. The views of picturesque Northeast Harbor are superb throughout. This

Opening the garden door, Thuya Garden

trail is perfect for families of divergent tastes and abilities.

From the junction of Route 3/198 and Route 3 in Northeast Harbor, drive 0.4 mile southeast on Route 3 to the parking lot for Thuya Garden on the right (ocean) side of the road. Park and walk across Route 3 to find the path leading up to Asticou Terraces, marked by a subtle carved sign just 50 feet to the right.

Follow the stone and gravel path as it climbs the steep, spruce-covered hillside. Landscape architect Joseph Curtis designed the unique Asticou Terraces with the utmost sensitivity for blending man-made structures with the beauty and grace of the natural mountainside. It is impossible to detect which trees and plants have been aesthetically placed and which occurred naturally in this location. Three rustic shelters constructed of harmonious materials and set unobtrusively into the hillside make the most of the beautiful ocean views.

There are many ways to meander up the terraces, and all paths lead to Thuya Garden. One recommended route is to follow the signs for the Curtis Memorial, taking a left off the main path. Arrive quickly at a stone terrace sheltering a bronze memorial to the skilled and generous architect. Take in the fine views opposite the plaque, then walk past the memorial to continue your ascent. Stay left at the next two intersections and rise to a handsome stone hut overlooking the harbor. Enjoy the comfortable wooden benches inside the lookout or, if the benches are already occupied, continue your hike. Do not fret, the best lookout awaits.

Return to the last intersection and resume your climb on art-fully placed granite steps. At the next junction, again take a left to visit the second view-filled gazebo. From this hut, reach a very special place by proceeding north across the blueberry- and juniper-covered ledge on a very faint trail. After a few hundred feet, reach the most remote gazebo, framed and hidden by lovely, long-needled red pine. It is a real coup to take your rest stop here, for many hikers have no idea this little gem exists. If someone is occupying the lookout, be content to have a seat on the sun-kissed ledge to enjoy the view.

To reach Thuya Garden, retrace your steps to the second hut, then return to the main trail and continue to ascend, crossing a rock bridge over a small, pretty stream. Climb up ledges to an unusual path of crushed pink granite in the shade of beautiful spruce and cedars. The pink path leads directly to the Thuya Lodge, the summerhouse of John Curtis, at approximately 0.5 mile from the trailhead. The lodge, housing a fine horticultural library, is open to visitors July through Labor Day.

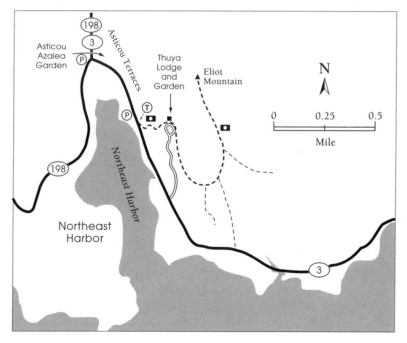

Most will want to proceed directly to Thuya Garden. Wonderfully carved wooden doors open to a beautiful formal garden. Paths lead past spacious lawns and long, colorful flower beds to intimate sitting areas. An especially fine wooden gazebo at the garden's north end inspires dreams of weddings as fanciful and romantic as fairy tales. Savor the cloistered feel of this tranquil place. The garden is especially magical when visited in the early morning or at dusk, when visitors are rare.

From here, you have the option of retracing your steps and returning to the trailhead for a round trip of 1 mile. Those continuing on to Eliot Mountain should follow the garden path to the southeast corner of the garden (the upper right-hand corner). Climb stairs to a door indicating the Eliot Mountain Trail. Leave the garden by this door and head south on the level path.

At the first intersection, turn left and climb over a moss- and berry-covered ledge. Quickly come to a second sign that simply indicates "Up!" (Someone has a sense of humor.) Walk through a beautiful mixed forest to yet another fork. Stay left. (The trail to the right descends to Route 3.) Follow small cairns, ascending a steep stretch that affords good views over Northeast Harbor. Again stay to the left at a third fork, and 1.1 miles from the trailhead, arrive at the top of Eliot Mountain, where there is a monument to Charles Eliot. Unfortunately, trees obscure your views at the summit.

On the trip back, regain excellent views as you retrace your steps to Thuya Garden. From the garden, amble back down the Asticou Terraces to the parking area.

If you still have a yen for garden walking, do not miss the nearby Asticou Azalea Garden where the Japanese-inspired design is particularly lovely and unique. The Azalea Garden is located about 100 yards north of the intersection of Routes 3/198 and 3, off Route 3/198. Alternatively, it is just a 0.5-mile walk west from the Thuya Garden parking area along Route 3 to reach the Azalea Garden. This side trip is highly recommended.

CHAPTER

3

Hiking Western Acadia National Park

Western Acadia National Park offers a diverse sampling of forest, summit, and ocean trails. The western side of Mount Desert Island is known as the quiet side, and often families find its trails less crowded and its small towns less hectic and tourist-driven. This region also offers fine camping opportunities, including Seaview Campground, Acadia National Park's most scenic campground. Other west-side attractions include the superlative Oceanarium in Southwest Harbor, the island's only self-guided seaside nature trail (trips 16, Ship Harbor Nature Trail, and 17, Wonderland Trail), and the gorgeous nature preserve at Indian Point where harbor seals frolic just offshore (trip 18, Indian Point Woods and Shore Trail).

For families seeking solitude on mountain summits, hikers are few and far between on Mansell and Bernard Mountains (trips 14 and 15). And although Beech Mountain attracts a fair number of visitors, the Beech Mountain Loop (trip 13) remains one of the most scenic and diverse hikes on Mount Desert Island.

------------------------ 13 ------------------------

Valley Trail and Beech Mountain Loop

TYPE: Hiking trail
DIFFICULTY: Moderate
DISTANCE: 2.9-mile loop
USAGE: Moderate
STARTING ELEVATION: 250 feet
HIGH POINT: 839 feet
SEASON: Spring, summer, fall

Children adore this moderately challenging hike because the terrain keeps changing and unusual wonders abound. It is especially

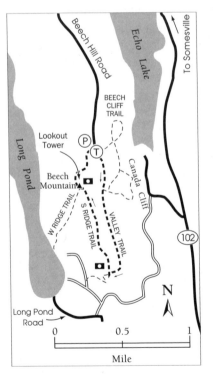

rich during wet summers when ferns, fungi, and moss create an almost mystical world of lilliputian beauty. For the first half of the hike, bring a magnifying glass to discover intricate forest wonders, then whip out binoculars to take in beautiful, sweeping vistas as you climb to an abandoned fire tower on the top of Beech Mountain. Also carry bug repellent, for the lush forest is home to abundant biting insects.

From the junction of Routes 198 and 102, just north of Somesville, drive south on Route 102 about 0.8 mile to the intersection with Route 102 heading west (also called Pretty Marsh Road). Turn right on Route 102 and drive 0.25 mile to Beech Hill

Road on the left. Turn left and proceed about 3.1 miles to the parking lot at the road's end. The trailhead for the Valley Trail is at the south end of the lot.

From the trailhead, plunge immediately into a shady, mixed forest. The wide, fairly level path runs in the trough between Canada Cliff to the east and the southern ridge of Beech Mountain to the west. With each step you take, these high cliffs appear taller, sweeping you into a new world.

And what a fascinating world it is! As far as the eye can see, aspen, birch, beech, maple, and fir surround the trail and climb the slopes on either side. Feathery ferns decorate the forest floor and colorful fungi pop from the ground like refugees from *Alice in Wonderland*. At your feet a thick carpet of moss in myriad shapes and colors covers all but the trail. Small streams run peacefully on both sides.

In just 0.2 mile, arrive at an intersection with the Canada Cliff Trail. Stay right. Walk carefully over roots and rocks (those covered by lichen are very slippery when wet). Descend by stone stairs. A deep, green ravine plunges to your left.

Soon arrive at one of the trail's most charming sections. Long ago, huge boulders fell from the looming cliffs above. Today the trail is surrounded by a magical jumble of moss-covered boulders. If a hobbit or troll were to live on this earth, he would undoubtedly choose this spot. Atop the boulders, rock cap ferns create comical hairdos. Other boulders are slathered with "rock tripe," a lichen considered tasty by the Japanese. In spring the rock tripe is green and full of moisture. By midsummer, it dries to resemble large, burnt corn flakes. Let the children explore this wonderland of shallow caves and secret places.

This is also an excellent place to discover the magical world of lichens and mosses. Kneel down to find gruesome "dead man's fingers," the skinny, light brown, fingerlike appendages that poke out above the green mats of moss. Look also for abundant reindeer moss, a silvery mass of delicately branched, tiny "antlers." Reindeer moss (really a lichen) is an important food source for arctic reindeer. The fragile lichen is an excellent indicator of air quality, for it cannot survive in areas of elevated carbon dioxide. Lastly, in places where the sun penetrates the canopy, look for tiny upright stalks with bright red caps, aptly named "british soldiers."

Beech Mountain summit

Back on the trail, descend stone steps and cross a small stream. Then rise gently through dense forest. At 0.8 mile from the trailhead, arrive at another fork and head right for Beech Mountain. Note the abundance of trees for which this mountain was named. Beech trees are easily recognized by their motley-looking gray bark, which is usually infected with a type of fungus. Beech trees produce a rough husked nut that is highly prized by squirrels.

The trail junction marks the beginning of your ascent. Climb steep granite steps that take you quickly up the mountainside. Ask children to count the stairs, and they will quickly forget the drudgery of climbing. As you gain altitude, switchback by switchback, the forest turns to spruce. Views of Long Pond appear to the southwest.

The stairs (177, I believe) finally end on a granite ledge. Fabulous, unobstructed views improve as the trail continues its climb. Look south to see the harbor and islands, and west to view the peaks of Mansell and Bernard. Follow blazes and cairns up and over a juniper-covered ledge. From mid-June to mid-July, the pretty pink flowers of sheep laurel, or lamb kill, adorn the granite. This plant is so named because it is poisonous to livestock. Abundant huckleberry and more silvery reindeer lichen also grow atop the ridge.

Soon the Beech Mountain Fire Lookout Tower comes into view. Follow the cairns to its base and pause to admire the extensive view in all directions. Until 1972, this fire tower served an area from Blue Hill Bay to Frenchman Bay. The summit's wide-open ledge is an excellent place for a picnic. Take out the binoculars and scan the sky for soaring peregrine falcons, eagles, and hawks. In the fall, Beech Mountain is an excellent spot from which to view the raptor migration.

For an exquisitely scenic return, find the descending trails to the left of the tower. There are two ways down. Take the trail to the left. It is 0.2 mile longer, but the views gained are certainly worth it. Immediately arrive at a junction with the West Ridge Trail, and stay right (do not descend via the West Ridge Trail).

This last 0.7 mile to the parking lot passes all too fast. Each step is filled with gorgeous views to the west and north. The long, blue expanse of Long Pond lies directly below, and nearly the entire western side of Mount Desert Island is spread before you. Drink in the views as the trail descends the northwest side of Beech Mountain. Pause often to scan the horizon or steal blueberries from the sun-kissed bushes. Finally reenter the woods in the last 0.2 mile and emerge at the north end of the parking lot where you parked your car.

14

Mansell Mountain

TYPE: Hiking trail
DIFFICULTY: Strenuous
DISTANCE: 3.3-mile loop
USAGE: Low
STARTING ELEVATION: 70 feet
HIGH POINT: 949 feet
SEASON: Spring, summer, fall

The Perpendicular Trail ascending Mansell Mountain is a most unusual trail. Where else can hikers climb a mountain via a granite spiral staircase composed of hundreds of moss-covered stairs? The

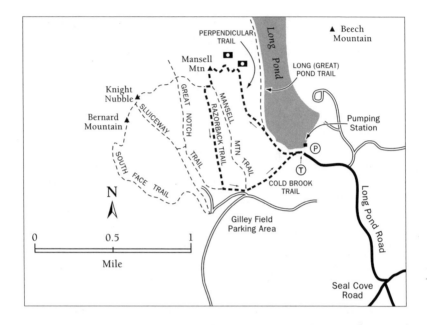

trail's elaborateness verges on the absurd, but its very eccentricity carries a certain beauty. Built by the Civilian Conservation Corps in the 1930s, the trail has aged well, and the stonecutters' passion now seems an integral part of Acadia's landscape. Best of all, the trail is wonderfully underused in this busy park, so lace up your boots (this trail is steep!), pack a lunch, and enjoy the marvelous views and well-earned solitude.

From Southwest Harbor, drive north on Route 102 about 0.7 mile to Seal Cove Road; from Somesville, drive south on Route 102 about 4.5 miles to Seal Cove Road. From either direction, turn west on Seal Cove Road and proceed 0.6 mile to Long Pond Road. Turn right and drive 1.2 miles to the road's end at the pumping station and parking lot at the south end of Long Pond. Park and find the trailhead just left (west) of the pumping station.

Follow the trail southwest along the pond's edge—the Great (Long) Pond Trail—and meet immediately a trail to the left signed for Mansell Mountain. Stay right. After 0.2 mile along the pond's edge, arrive at the junction with the Perpendicular Trail. Head left and begin your ascent up the carefully laid granite stairs. Rise under deliciously fragrant cedar and spruce, with dashes of maple that create bursts of color in the fall.

Switchback through forest, then ascend a rock slide on more artfully placed stairs. Good views of the pond soon appear. Master a particularly steep section with the help of three iron rungs and a short ladder. Rise just a bit further to gain perfectly gorgeous views to the south and east. Consider this spot for a sunrise picnic to watch the color appear over Southwest Harbor.

The mood of the trail changes as you follow it through forest. Cross a small stream and follow cairns, blazes, and blue metal flags. Climb a steep and eroded slope and look for a rock outcropping to the right of the trail. Carefully climb atop the outcropping for fabulous views west across the pond to Beech Mountain (spot the fire tower) and south to the Eastern Way and offshore islands. Then follow the trail as it swings to the left (west) into a thick stand of spruce, and descend to a moist, green garden of moss and grasses. The path then climbs to reach the viewless summit of Mansell at 949 feet, 1.2 miles from the trailhead.

From the summit head briefly north, following cairns and blue flags on a well-defined, gently descending trail. At 0.1 mile from

Handholds help young climbers up steep slopes.

the summit, arrive at an intersection with the Mansell Mountain Trail to the left. Stay to the right (west). The post indicates you are heading toward Knight Nubble and Bernard Mountain.

Immediately gain good views to the west, but watch your step as the trail drops extremely steeply. Then rise up a rocky knoll to meet the intersection with the Razorback Trail, just 0.2 mile from the Mansell summit. Turn left (south) to descend the Razorback Trail, immediately gaining fine views to the south and west. Follow cairns and watch for one steep drop where youngsters may need assistance.

Enjoy terrific but fleeting views as the trail quickly loses altitude. Soon the steep trail plunges into a shady forest. After 1.2 miles on Razorback, arrive at its intersection with the Cold Brook Trail. Turn left on Cold Brook, cross a bridge, and in 0.2 mile meet a parking lot at Gilley Field. Pick up the Cold Brook Trail on the other side of the lot and proceed northeast another 0.4 mile to Long Pond on the shady, root-strewn trail.

At the edge of Long Pond, arrive at an intersection with the Great (Long) Pond Trail. Turn right and walk just 0.1 mile to the pumping station and parking lot where the hike began.

15

Bernard Mountain

> TYPE: Hiking Trail
> DIFFICULTY: Moderate
> DISTANCE: 1.6 miles one way
> USAGE: Low
> STARTING ELEVATION: 100 feet
> HIGH POINT: 1,071 feet
> SEASON: Spring, summer, fall

Ascend the west ridge of Bernard Mountain for some fine views, solitude, and a chance to enter the darkest, quietest forest on Mount Desert Island. The recently reopened West Ridge Trail has not yet had a chance to gain a loyal following. In fall you may have the colorful slopes and Merlinesque forest all to yourself.

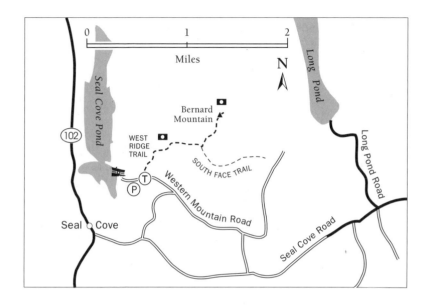

From Seal Cove on the west side of Mount Desert Island, drive south on Route 102 less than 0.1 mile to Seal Cove Road. Turn left, drive approximately 0.5 mile, and turn left. Drive about 0.5 mile until you reach Western Mountain Road. Turn left on Western Mountain Road and proceed 0.3 mile to a small turnout on the left side of the road.

From Southwest Harbor, drive north on Route 102 about 0.7 mile to Seal Cove Road (from Somesville, drive south on Route 102 about 4.5 miles to Seal Cove Road). Drive approximately 2.5 miles west on Seal Cove Road and turn right. Drive about 0.3 mile to the intersection with Western Mountain Road. Turn left on Western Mountain Road and proceed 1.4 miles until you see a small turnout on the left side of the road.

The parking turnout is 0.2 mile east of the boat launch at Seal Cove Pond. Park and walk across the street to the trailhead marked by a cedar post.

Follow the trail as it climbs fairly steeply over a ledge marked by cairns. Abundant blueberry and delicate mosses soften the rocky slope. As you climb, maple and aspen give way to spruce.

The trail drops, then climbs in earnest up a steep rock outcropping. Your efforts are rewarded by excellent views to the south of Blue Hill Bay and west to pretty Seal Cove Pond. Continue to climb, for the views improve as you gain altitude. Pass through several wooded sections, emerging each time to a grander, view-filled ledge. The open granite ledge provides an abundance of excellent picnic spots.

At 1.1 miles from the trailhead, arrive at the junction with the South Ridge Trail. Take the left fork (straight ahead) for Bernard Mountain summit, 0.5 mile away.

The mood of the trail changes dramatically as you enter a dark and quiet old-growth spruce-fir forest. A thick carpet of needles covers the forest floor. Scattered patches of green moss provide the only color. Because the upper branches of the trees block out most of the sunlight, the needleless lower branches reach out brittle and lifeless, giving the thick forest a mysterious primeval feel. As you near the summit, more young trees and sunlight penetrate, and the forest becomes quite beautiful.

In 1.3 miles from the trailhead, reach the forested summit of Bernard Mountain at 1,071 feet. For views, follow the trail just 5 minutes further to reach an open area with terrific views to the north.

To return to the trailhead, simply retrace your steps.

Dogs on trails must be kept on a leash no longer than 6 feet!

16

Ship Harbor Nature Trail

TYPE: Self-guided hiking trail
DIFFICULTY: Easy
DISTANCE: 1.3-mile loop
USAGE: High
STARTING ELEVATION: Sea level
HIGH POINT: 75 feet
SEASON: Year-round

This easy, self-guided nature trail along Ship Harbor to the ocean shore is an excellent introduction to coastal ecology. Its trail booklet (available at the visitor center and from a dispenser at the trailhead) provides brief descriptions corresponding to numbered stations along the path. Arrive at low tide for fascinating tide pooling (bring a small, clear plastic container for temporarily housing sea creatures) or attend a special ranger-led hike geared to families (check at the visitor center for details). This trail can also be combined with the Wonderland Trail (see trip 17) to create a 2.5-mile loop with plenty of rock-hopping and ocean viewing.

From Southwest Harbor, drive south on Route 102 about 0.6 mile to the junction of Routes 102 and 102A. Bear left and take Route 102A 4.25 miles (1.25 miles past Seawall Campground) to a parking area on the left side of the road signed for the Ship Harbor Nature Trail. Find the trail at the south end of the parking area.

Purchase a trail guide and head southeast on the well-marked trail. At the fork in the trail, bear left to follow the trail guide sequentially. (The trail makes a looping figure eight, so those bearing right will also end up at the ocean's shore.) At the next junction in the trail (the center of the figure eight), bear left.

As you near the ocean, white spruce becomes the dominant tree. Recognize white spruce by its sharp green needles that appear square in cross section. Shake hands with a spruce to feel its spiky needles. To be sure you are shaking a white spruce (and not a red spruce), check the color of the needles. White spruce needles are whitish due to a thick coating of wax. The wax protects the

Ranger-led walks are popular on the Ship Harbor Nature Trail.

needles from salt mist and fog, enabling the trees to thrive close to the sea where other trees would perish. If you are still not sure, a dead giveaway for identifying a white spruce is to crush a few needles. If they smell like skunk, you have found a white spruce!

Shortly, the trail emerges at the ocean 0.6 mile from the trailhead, providing hikers with a wide expanse of rocky shoreline to explore. At low tide, rock ledges trap pockets of seawater. These pools offer a close-up view of many sea creatures and plants. Walk carefully over the rocks (black algae is very slippery), and choose a tide pool to explore. Use a plastic container partially filled with seawater to gently place sea creatures for close observation. By using a clear container, the creatures can be seen from every angle and handling is kept to a minimum. By placing them in water, the creatures can move about naturally.

What are you likely to find? First, notice the barnacles that cover the rocks, both above and below the tide pools. Barnacles barely look like living animals, yet they are actually crustaceans related to crabs and lobsters. Cemented by the thousands to the rocks, they more closely resemble dime-size volcanoes. To discover what barnacles are really like, find a few below the surface of the tide pool. Wave your hand in front of the barnacles (to simulate the movement of the tide) and watch carefully as six pairs of feathery legs come out and wave in the water. Since the barnacle's neck is forever cemented to the rock, it uses its legs to sweep food (tiny plankton) into its mouth.

You are also likely to see an abundance of winkles. These tiny snails are usually no bigger than a quarter. Their shells come in a variety of attractively whorled colors, from brown to yellow-orange. Picking up a periwinkle will cause it to retreat quickly into its shell. Humming softly toward the shell often brings the shy winkle out for a look!

Other creatures commonly found in Acadia's tide pools are crabs, mussels, and sea stars. Watch out if you find a small green crab, for despite their tiny size (1 to 3 inches), these crabs can pinch! Less testy are the hermit crabs, which produce no hard shell of their own and must live in the empty and discarded shells of other snails. Purplish-black mussels are also found everywhere attached to the rocks.

Lucky tide poolers may also find one of Acadia's two types of sea stars (or starfish), the more common "purple" or the tiny, bright red "blood" sea star. Both are fascinating creatures. Should a sea star lose one of its five arms, it can usually grow another!

Lastly, do not forget to look at the wonderful variety of plants in and around the tide pools. The long, thin strands of green seaweed in the pools are called mermaid's hair. The slippery green plant with air bladders is rock weed or bladder wrack. When the water covers the rocks at high tide, the air bladders help the rock weed stand vertically in the water. Twice a day, at low tide, the entire forest of rock weed lies down on the rocks. Carefully lift a bunch of rock weed. You may uncover the periwinkles that love to dine on it, or the little green crabs that hide under it. Finally, especially if you are hungry, look for a slimy reddish purple plant with large rounded lobes called dulse. Dried dulse is a popular Japanese snack. Tear off a little piece and taste it. Its salty taste is really very pleasant!

After tide pooling (*and* after gently returning all creatures to their original places), hikers have two options. To enjoy a longer walk along the coast, proceed along the rocks north to the Wonderland Trail (trip 17). This trip adds approximately 1.25 miles

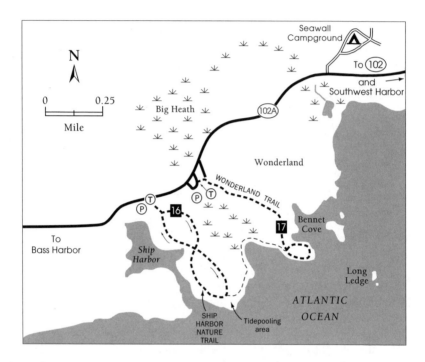

to the total hiking distance. Those who wish to return more directly must retrace their steps to the point where the Ship Harbor Nature Trail entered the shore, and follow it southwest to continue the self-guided hike. Those opting to hike north to visit Wonderland should retrace their steps after visiting Wonderland and regain the Ship Harbor Nature Trail at this point.

The second half of the nature trail follows the shore of shallow Ship Harbor. At low tide, this area is composed mostly of mudflats. The area got its name during the Revolutionary War when a ship sailed into the inlet to escape a pursuing British vessel and ran aground. At the edge of the mudflats grows salt marsh hay, which early settlers harvested and shipped south for sale at Boston's famous Haymarket (the market still exists, though a rich variety of produce replaced the hay). Hikers may also notice delicate flowering sea lavender. This plant is much prized for dried flower arrangements, but it is against park regulations to pick it.

At the next trail junction (the center of the figure eight), stay left. The trail proceeds along the "harbor," then through mixed forest to arrive at the path from the parking lot. At the junction with this path, bear left and reach your car after 0.1 mile.

17

Wonderland Trail

TYPE: Hiking trail
DIFFICULTY: Easy (handicapped-accessible with
  assistance)
DISTANCE: 0.7 mile one way
USAGE: High
STARTING ELEVATION: 30 feet
HIGH POINT: 35 feet
SEASON: Year-round

Arrive at low tide with a picnic in hand for the effortless excursion to aptly named Wonderland. There you will find an unusual beach covered in smooth blocks of granite, providing perfect places to play, explore, tide pool, and picnic. Located on the edge of Bennet Cove, Wonderland is wonderfully accessible, yet far from the busy roads and crowds of the Park Loop Road. Hikers can even take a stroller, for the trail follows an old gravel fire road for the entire distance to the beach. To extend this easy hike to a 2.5-mile loop, combine this walk with the Ship Harbor Nature Trail (trip 16) just 0.6 mile to the south. Note, however, that neither the rocky coast itself nor the Ship Harbor Nature Trail is accessible to strollers or wheelchairs.

From Southwest Harbor, drive south on Route 102 about 0.6 mile to the junction of Routes 102 and 102A. Bear left and take Route 102A approximately 4 miles (1 mile past the Seawall Campground) to a parking area on the left side of the road, marked by a park service sign indicating WONDERLAND. Find the start of the trail at the southeast end of the parking lot.

The trail soon merges with the gravel road that enters from the left. Stroll southeast down the gravel road. Hikers can either head straight down the road to the beach or explore the many very short spur trails that leave the road to wander in soft, green, boggy gardens. These luxurious spaces hold much fascination for youngsters. Let them investigate (with the utmost respect for plants and creatures) the trampolinelike ground, round moss "fairy beds," dewy orb spider webs, green caterpillars, tickling ferns, and trees clothed in furry moss "sweaters."

Tidepooling

After approximately 0.5 mile, meet a fork in the road. Stay right and reach the shore in a few quick steps, passing a profusion of rugosa rose and raspberry bushes. In late summer these shrubs hang heavy with delicious fruit for the island's winged and human visitors.

Arrive at the beach and you have reached Wonderland, a phantasmagoric jungle of granite blocks tumbling to the water's edge. Youngsters love to climb and jump from rock to rock. For parents, there are infinite places to spread a picnic among the fallen Stonehenge-like boulders. If you have come at low tide, investigate the many tide pools trapped in the pockets between the rocks. For a detailed description of the plants and creatures you are likely to encounter, see trip 16, Ship Harbor Nature Trail.

When you are ready to leave the beach, continue walking north to catch the second half of the road's loop. Walking northwest, you will pass Bennet Cove, which also provides interesting places to explore at low tide. Proceed around the loop to the main road and retrace your steps to reach the parking lot.

Those who wish to extend their hike to include the Ship Harbor Nature Trail (located 0.6 mile to the south along the coast) should walk south along the rocky shore (there is no specific trail) to the tip of the next point of land where the end of the Ship Harbor

Nature Trail meets the shore. At this junction, hikers should turn inland and follow the directions in trip 16. If hikers know in advance that they want to hike the 2.5-mile loop, it is recommended that they begin at Ship Harbor and walk north along the coast to visit Wonderland, because they will be better able to take advantage of the self-guided nature trail.

18

Indian Point Woods and Shore Trail

TYPE: Hiking trail
DIFFICULTY: easy
DISTANCE: 1.1 miles one way
USAGE: Moderate
STARTING ELEVATION: Sea level
HIGH POINT: Sea level
SEASON: Year-round

The delightful Indian Point–Blagden Preserve enchants children of all ages. Enjoy its beautiful parklike setting, the brevity of its level trails, and, above all, the sight of harbor seals on the preserve's offshore islands. With binoculars, you can often spot seals sunning on the nearby ledges or frolicking in the water. This exceptionally scenic property on the Indian Point Peninsula on the northwest side of Mount Desert Island is owned and managed by The Nature Conservancy, an international conservation organization. Accordingly, please respect the conservancy's rules of use: pets, picnicking, and boat launching are prohibited, and the preserve closes at 6 P.M.

From Bar Harbor, drive west on Route 233 about 5.8 miles to the junction of Routes 198 and 3/198. Bear right at this junction on Route 198 and proceed 1.4 miles in a westerly direction to the junction with Route 102 to Somesville and Route 102/198 heading north. Turn left toward Somesville on Route 102 and proceed about 0.4 mile to Oak Hill Road and turn right. Drive about 2.1 miles on Oak Hill Road to its intersection with Indian Point Road. Turn left on Indian Point Road and immediately look for

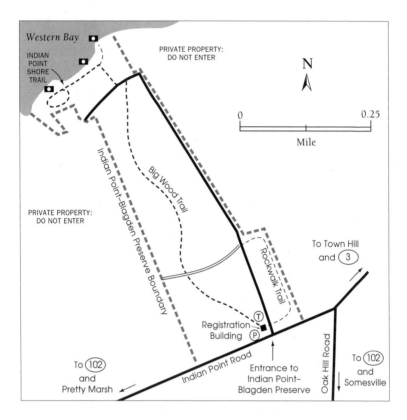

the entrance to the Indian Point Preserve about 200 yards on the right, marked by a small sign. Turn right into the preserve, and find the parking lot immediately to your left. Sign in at the building adjacent to the lot.

From the parking lot, it's an easy 0.75-mile walk to the shore. Hikers can take the Big Woods Trail, a pleasant path that meanders north through young woods. It is also possible to follow the paved road, which is now closed to vehicular traffic. After three-quarters of a mile, both reach the start of the Shore Trail on the north side of the road (just after the road bends to the west).

The Shore Trail makes a short loop along the tip of the Indian Point peninsula, skirting the preserve's exquisitely beautiful frontage on Western Bay. You may be distracted by the inviting site of freshly painted Adirondack chairs set in advantageous spots along the shore. These chairs are yours to enjoy, and a more convivial spot on Mount Desert Island is hard to find. If you can, however, resist the temptation to park yourself immediately, and follow first the brief and effortless Shore Trail.

The Shore Trail leads through ferns and bunchberry across a red wooden bridge. Be sure to stay on the narrow trail, as there is plenty of poison ivy nearby. Arrive at a fork, go right, and pass through fine spruces to emerge on the shore. After a few minutes' walk along the rocky coastline, come to the end of the preserve. Please honor the signs, and do not trespass on private property. The ability of The Nature Conservancy to welcome public use depends on visitors' respect for the abutter's privacy. To finish the Shore Trail Loop, follow the path into the shady spruce forest. The path simply circles through the woods and returns to the main trail.

After exploring, choose a favorite spot along the rocky shoreline and take out your binoculars. You may wish to hike further north up the shoreline, where there are additional chairs and flat rocks. Look for harbor seals on and around the several small islands that lie just offshore. The seals are most readily seen in spring and early summer when they come to the ledges to bear their young. Seals do, nevertheless, remain near Indian Point year-round.

Tides also affect seal activity. When the tide is falling, seals often bask on the exposed ledges or mudflats. At high tide, they are usually in the water hunting for food. Recognize harbor seals by their chubby yet streamlined bodies, with mottled coats ranging from light gray to brownish black. The harbor seal's large eyes and short, rounded muzzle earn them the name "sea dog," for in the water their bobbing heads resemble a labrador retriever's. Gray seals, on the other hand, are a rare sight at Indian Point. Gray seals are much larger than harbor seals and have a longer nose and more pronounced nostrils. Their nickname is "horsehead."

If you spot a seal on the shore, especially a seal pup, do not approach. Approaching too closely will cause the seal to experience stress and may harm the seal's health. If a seal rears its head or acts nervous, retreat immediately. If a seal appears to be injured, notify a park ranger.

If you do not see seals, plan to return another day at low tide. Or just relax, take in a sunset over Western Bay, and look for the osprey and bald eagles that also frequent the area. For more information on the good works of The Nature Conservancy, see appendix C, Conservation Organizations.

CHAPTER

4

Hiking Isle au Haut and the Schoodic Peninsula

In addition to the tens of thousands of acres of national parklands located on Mount Desert Island, Acadia National Park also includes two particularly beautiful and pristine properties: the remote island of Isle au Haut and the unspoiled point of land known as the Schoodic Peninsula. Although reaching these areas requires a moderate amount of time and effort, the rewards are tremendous. Visitors to these special places can discover the true wildness, grandeur, and beauty of the Maine coast. The hiking opportunities on Isle au Haut and the Schoodic Peninsula are unequaled.

The Schoodic Peninsula is easily reached by driving approximately 45 miles from Bar Harbor. The two featured hikes on the peninsula include an easy walk to an island connected to the mainland only at low tide (trip 19, Little Moose Island) and a challenging climb to the peninsula's highest point through dense, primeval forest (trip 20, Anvil Trail). Visit the Schoodic Peninsula at dawn or dusk, and whitetail deer or moose may surprise you. Arrive on a stormy day, and experience crashing waves in full fury.

A visit to Isle au Haut requires a bit more planning, but it is equally worthwhile. The island is located about 5 miles south of Stonington, which is a 60-mile drive from Bar Harbor. From Stonington, hikers must travel to the island by mail boat (see "Camping" in Planning Your Trip Is Essential, chapter 1).

French explorer Samuel Champlain named Isle au Haut "High Island" for the range of mountains running along its 6-mile length. Acadia National Park occupies roughly the southern half of the island, while the northern half is occupied by summer residents and a year-round fishing community. Eighteen miles of trail traverse the parkland, offering superb hiking opportunities. Explore rocky coastline and wooded uplands (trip 21, Western Head and Cliff Trails) or climb 314-foot Duck Harbor Mountain (trip 22, Goat Trail and Duck Harbor Mountain Trail). Hiking is wonderfully uncrowded on Isle au Haut, because the National Park Service limits the number of daily visitors arriving on the island. In addition, Isle au Haut's tiny but beautiful campground at Duck Harbor offers superlative family camping (see chapter 1).

19

Little Moose Island

TYPE: Hiking trail
DIFFICULTY: Easy
DISTANCE: 1.3 miles one way
USAGE: Low
STARTING ELEVATION: Sea level
HIGH POINT: 70 feet
SEASON: Spring, summer, fall

For sweeping ocean vistas and welcome solitude, this short hike to Little Moose Island is unequaled. Timing is everything, however, for the island is only accessible to hikers at low tide when a gravel beach connects the island to the mainland. When the tide is out, hikers can walk across the beach and explore the scrubby highlands of the tiny island. Informal trails lead to spectacular views, ledges for picnicking, and great beaches for treasure hunting.

The Schoodic Peninsula is located about 45 miles from Bar Harbor, and the drive takes nearly an hour. From Bar Harbor, take Route 3 north about 18 miles to the junction of Route 3 and US 1 in Ellsworth. Turn right (east) on US 1 and drive 17.1 miles to its junction with Route 186 in West Gouldsboro. Turn right (south) on Route 186. Drive about 8.5 miles on Route 186, through Winter Harbor. About 0.6 mile east of Winter Harbor, turn right off Route 186 onto Moore Road, which loops around the Schoodic Peninsula. The entrance to Acadia National Park is 1.3 miles ahead.

From the peninsula's park entrance, drive past the Frazer Point Picnic Area where the road becomes one-way. From the start of the one-way road, drive 2.9 miles to a fork, where the road to the right goes out to Schoodic Point. Stay left and drive 0.2 mile past the fork to a point in the road just across from Little Moose Island. There is room for a couple of cars to pull off.

Begin the hike by walking across the gravel bar to Little Moose Island. In summer the island is covered with seaside rose bushes sporting showy pink blossoms *(Rosa rugosa)*. Stroll along the rocky beach on the western side of Little Moose Island. Visible just across Arey Cove to the west is Schoodic Point. Little Moose beach is a treasure trove of sun-bleached driftwood, shells, rocks, and sundry items discarded by the sea. Youngsters can create impromptu teeter-totters or balance beams from the large wood

A driftwood seesaw on Little Moose Island

planks that litter the beach.

Next, locate the NPS sign to find the trail that leaves the beach on a narrow path and heads south. Make your way by trail and granite ledge to the southern tip of the island where cliffs fall precipitously to the sea, about 0.6 mile from the trailhead. Wedged between the rocks grow tenacious blue harebells, a delicate bluish purple bell-shaped flower that blooms from mid-July to September. True to its name, the harebell is a favorite food of snowshoe hares, the only type of rabbit found in the park. Step only on rocks, and spare the fragile vegetation that grows on the island. Little Moose Island is a haven for several rare plants. The state of Maine has recognized it as a Critical Area for its botanic values. When the wind is calm, the granite ledges at the end of the island make a fine spot for a picnic. When the ocean is angry, there are few better spots to watch its fury.

The island's edge is also a good place to observe seabirds. Watch the waves for bobbing groups of lovely eider ducks. The handsome males are formally attired in striking black and white (black cap and mask, white back and breast, black wings and tail). Their remarkable good looks were nearly the demise of the species. In the early 1900s, eider feathers were in such demand for ladies' hats that hunting almost caused their extinction. Sometimes the entire bird was mounted on the hat! Although today it is common to see large rafts (groups) of eiders along the coast, in 1936 the park service could document only *two* pairs of breeding eiders. Fortunately, protective legislation and public awareness saved the species.

Watch also for a smaller black duck, the guillemot. Also called sea pigeons, guillemots are remarkable in their ability to use their small wings to swim underwater. They pursue fish and crustaceans to depths of 165 feet! Guillemots are related to auks and puffins, and are entirely black, except for white wing patches. Lucky close-up observers may see their bright red feet and red mouth lining.

To leave the island, retrace your steps down the meandering, narrow trail. The view inland from the island is beautiful, filled with mountains both near and far. On the way back, you will notice numerous spur trails crisscrossing the island. Stay on the main trail to avoid trampling the rare and fragile vegetation. This is a very special place.

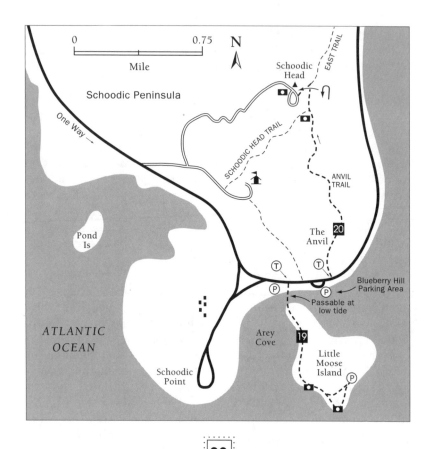

Anvil Trail

TYPE: Hiking trail
DIFFICULTY: Moderate
DISTANCE: 1 mile one way
USAGE: Low
STARTING ELEVATION: 50 feet
HIGH POINT: 440 feet
SEASON: Spring, summer, fall

Experience the coastal forest primeval in all its glory on the Anvil
Trail. This is one of the few trails in Acadia that lack a well-kept,

manicured feel, and it is fabulous! Hikers ascend a rough, narrow path through spruce dripping with moss, amid huge boulders shrouded with lichen, to Schoodic Head, the highest point on the Schoodic Peninsula. The views are spectacular, but the most fun is the scramble up the strange rocky knoll called "The Anvil" and the journey through the mystically beautiful forest. Do not let fog be a deterrent; the forest is even more magical when it is softly cloaked in gray mist. Keep eyes and ears tuned for moose and whitetail deer, for they frequent the peninsula. The park service plans to improve the trail in 1997.

Follow the driving directions for trip 19, Little Moose Island. Continue past the trailhead for Little Moose Island about 0.3 mile to the Blueberry Hill parking area. Park here and walk up the road approximately 0.1 mile to the trailhead marked by a wooden marker on the left side of the road. (There is a pullout for a couple of cars almost opposite the trailhead.)

From the trail marker, pass through blueberry bushes, then follow blue blazes into the forest. Rich green moss hangs from every branch, and lichen covers every surface in all imaginable shades of green. Watch for roots (slippery when wet) that stud the trail. This forest envelops you; only the low rumbling of surf penetrates its silence.

Almost immediately, the trail rises. Climb past huge boulders where lichen grows inches thick. Among the different varieties are reindeer moss and rock tripe lichen. Recognize reindeer moss by its silvery branches that look like tiny antlers. Rock tripe lichen, in contrast, resembles large, burnt cornflakes. In Asia, rock tripe is gathered for food. It has a peppery taste and is often added to soups. Native Americans saw this lichen quite differently. They named it after a wood nymph whose lips had been burned off. Strangely, the rock tripe's papery, brown layers resemble absurdly thin, grotesquely shaped lips.

After about 0.3 mile, arrive at The Anvil, a mysterious rocky knoll shaped like a tall granite amphitheater. This is a good place to do a little exploring. For the youngest hikers, this may be a good turnaround point, for the remainder of the hike involves a fair amount of climbing.

While exploring the immediate area, look for evidence of deer and moose. Moose tracks are surprisingly large (about 6½ inches long for a large bull) and roundish. In contrast, deer tracks are much smaller (about 3 inches long for a mature buck) and more

Forest, moss, lichen, and boulders on the Anvil Trail

pointed, almost heart-shaped. If you are lucky enough to spot either animal, you should appreciate them from a distance, and do not approach. Both have an exceptionally keen sense of hearing and are likely to move off rapidly once they discern your presence. In addition, both animals can be aggressive, especially when accompanied by their young or during the mating season.

To continue to Schoodic Head, keep climbing, looking carefully for blue blazes. The Anvil Trail climbs generally in a northerly direction, twisting and turning around trees and boulders. Near the top of Schoodic Head, cross a little stone bridge over a narrow crevice. Then curve to the left and arrive at a cairn denoting an overlook. Walk carefully to the overlook, located at the edge of a cliff. The overlook offers spectacular views east over Winter Harbor and toward the mountains of Mount Desert Island.

Fog often obscures this view. Unfortunately, Acadia's fog may not always be benign. Although there is relatively little air pollution generated within the park, acid precipitation in Acadia has been measured at ten times normal levels. This pollution is produced primarily in eastern cities and is carried into the park by air currents. Scientists have found that acid fog is the most acidic form of acid precipitation, and it frequently blankets Maine forests. This fog may contribute to the needle injury found on red spruce and the increased acidity of some lakes and ponds. Whether in the park or at home, your efforts to conserve energy will help to reduce air pollution and its adverse effects, both near and far.

After enjoying the overlook, arrive at a trail junction 0.8 mile from the trailhead with the Schoodic Head Trail that approaches from the south (left). Continue north (right) and descend briefly, then climb approximately 0.1 mile to a trail junction with the East Trail. Turn left to reach Schoodic Head after another 0.1 mile. On Schoodic Head, you'll meet an unpaved road that runs from the ranger station located southwest of the summit. At the summit, enjoy fine views of the peninsula before retracing your steps to return to the trailhead.

21

Western Head and Cliff Trails

TYPE: Hiking trail
DIFFICULTY: Moderate
DISTANCE: 4.1-mile loop
USAGE: Low
STARTING ELEVATION: Sea level
HIGH POINT: 100 feet
SEASON: Spring, summer, fall

This easy family hike skirts the unspoiled and spectacular southern shoreline of Isle au Haut. Narrow passages through dark spruce forest connect high, dramatic headlands and isolated stony beaches. Enjoy a wealth of panoramic ocean vistas featuring sea-birds, lobster boats, and crashing waves. Bring a picnic to savor amid the abundance of magnificent scenery. Adventurous hikers can combine this trail with the Duck Harbor Mountain Trail (trip 22) to create an immensely scenic and challenging loop, perfect for a full day's hike.

Isle au Haut is accessible only by mail boat. Detailed travel information is given in chapter 1, in the Camping section of Planning Your Trip Is Essential. For trips 21 and 22, disembark at the Duck Harbor Landing (not at the Town Landing, where the ranger station is located). During the summer, a ranger boards the boat at the Town Landing to answer questions about the island and its trails.

After arriving at Duck Harbor, climb up the narrow trail from the dock to meet Western Head Road, a wide, grassy "road" no longer used for auto traffic. Head south on the road. Blueberry and sweet fern grow profusely at its borders. Recognize sweet fern

Playing in a natural sculpture on the Cliff Trail

(not a true fern, though it resembles one) by rubbing its leaflets gently between your hands. The perfumy scent on your palms indicate you have massaged a sweet fern. Early settlers used the plant to scent candles and soaps.

Arrive soon at a junction with the Duck Harbor Mountain Trail on the left. Stay right and continue rising gently up Western Head Road. After approximately 0.7 mile from the boat dock, reach a junction with the Western Head Trail on the right. Leave Western Head Road and turn right (southwest) onto the narrow trail. Watch your footing as the root-studded trail heads downhill through lush spruce forest. Log boardwalks and bridges keep feet dry as the trail crosses marshy areas and streams.

After about 0.4 mile, follow blue blazes to climb from the wet forest. The trail emerges dramatically at the ocean's edge, where a wide sweep of the island's rugged western coast is suddenly visible. Saddleback Ledge Lighthouse sits a few miles offshore. A bare ledge provides an excellent perch from which to catch your breath and contemplate the beautiful scene.

The trail next travels along the ocean's edge for more than a mile, visiting a delightful series of stony beaches and view-filled headlands. At the beaches, old buoys and driftwood of every shape and size provide creative hikers with raw material for sculptures. Many have been inspired. "Installations" at the time of this writing included spruces adorned with buoys like Christmas trees and planks set up like tables and "set" for tea with shell plates, stick silverware, and other imaginative garnishes. Youngsters will have fun treasure hunting and building their own fanciful sculptures.

Follow cairns and blazes as the trail delves in and out of dark, moss-covered spruce forest, always to emerge at another pebbly cove or headland. The trail climbs from beach to headland, affording hikers sweeping views of the coast. As the trail rounds the southern tip of Isle au Haut, a small spruce-covered island, called Western Ear, becomes visible just off the coast.

At 1.3 miles from the beginning of the Western Head Trail, arrive at the junction where the Cliff Trail heads off to the left. At low tide, hikers can visit the tiny island of Western Ear by turning right at this junction and walking across the exposed stony tidelands. Views of Isle au Haut are quite nice from Western Ear. (If you are wondering, there *is* also an Eastern Ear, which lies just east of Isle au Haut's Eastern Head!) Visitors must keep track of the incoming tide to avoid getting stranded and must abide by all posted restrictions, as Western Ear is privately owned.

Those continuing on the Cliff Trail head north and travel once more in and out of forest to headlands and rocky coves. The views are spectacular at each turn. About 0.7 mile from the junction with the Western Head Trail, the Cliff Trail climbs very steeply to emerge atop a magnificent bluff towering almost 100 feet above the water. The trail then descends to meet the south end of the Western Head Road in just 0.1 mile.

To return most expeditiously to the ferry dock, turn left onto Western Head Road and walk an easy and mostly level 1.4 miles back to the boat dock.

Alternatively, hikers can retrace their steps along the Cliff and Western Head Trails and return to the dock by this longer, more scenic route. Backtracking adds approximately 1.3 miles to the hike.

A third alternative is to make a wider loop and include a portion of the scenic coastal Goat Trail, then head inland on the Duck Harbor Mountain Trail and climb over Duck Harbor Mountain to reach the dock. This strenuous route is described in trip 22 and adds about 0.4 mile and an additional elevation gain of about 300 feet.

22

Goat Trail and Duck Harbor Mountain Trail

TYPE: Hiking trail
DIFFICULTY: Strenuous
DISTANCE: 3.6-mile loop
USAGE: Low
STARTING ELEVATION: Sea level
HIGH POINT: 314 feet
SEASON: Spring, summer, fall

This hike combines the most scenic portions of the ocean-side Goat Trail with a challenging and view-filled ascent of Duck Harbor

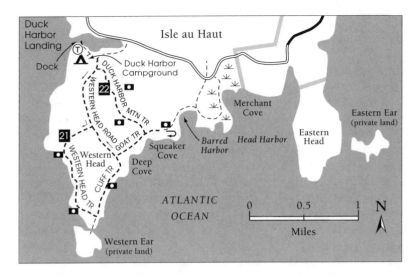

Mountain, Isle au Haut's southernmost peak. Duck Harbor Mountain is a fun mountain to climb. A succession of "puddings" (ledgy knobs) leads up to its summit, requiring a fair amount of four-point rock scrambling and fanny descents. Youngsters will need help, but they will enjoy the ride. Parents will appreciate the good views that prevail throughout the climb. For a terrifically scenic, but challenging, day hike, combine this hike with the Western Head and Cliff Trails (trip 21) for a total round-trip distance of 4.5 miles.

Those opting for the shorter loop should follow the directions for trip 21 to the intersection of Western Head Road and the Western Head Trail. Do not turn right, however, onto the Western Head Trail, but continue straight up the fairly level Western Head Road through verdant spruce forest for another 0.5 mile until its intersection with the Goat Trail on the left. Take a left onto the Goat Trail.

To hike the 4.5-mile scenic loop, follow the directions for trip 21 to the Cliff Trail's intersection with Western Head Road, about 2.7 miles from the ferry dock. Turn left onto Western Head Road and then, after only 0.1 mile, arrive at the road's intersection with the Goat Trail. Turn right onto the Goat Trail.

From Western Head Road, the Goat Trail travels briefly through forest, then along the edge of Deep Cove. At the north end of the cove, cross a stream and head into a dense stand of spruce.

The convergence of the branches overhead, the forest's filtered light, and the hushed stillness of the woods recall a gothic chapel. Follow the rolling forest path and arrive in 0.3 mile at the junction with the Duck Harbor Mountain Trail on the left.

Before beginning the climb, continue just a bit on the Goat Trail for some unbeatable ocean scenery. Visit first an unusually narrow and lovely bay called Squeaker Cove. Hemmed in by high granite ledges, the round wave-washed rocks "squeak" against one another as the water pounds into the narrow cove. Follow the Goat Trail as it re-enters moss-covered woods and climbs rather steeply to emerge high above the sea. Enter woods once more, cross a stream, then finally arrive on a ledge 100 feet above the ocean. The views are expansive and magnificent, particularly of Squeaker Cove and points west. From this vantage point, if the ocean is angry, the waves rushing into Squeaker Cove create a sound and fury similar to Acadia's infamous Thunder Hole. The beauty is that here, as opposed to busy Thunder Hole, there are no crowds, cars, or viewing lines.

After taking in the sights and refreshing breezes, return to the Goat Trail's junction with the Duck Harbor Mountain Trail by retracing your steps about 0.3 mile. At the junction, turn right (north) onto the Duck Harbor Mountain Trail to begin the ascent. Follow cairns that lead nearly straight up the mountain to your first pudding, and enjoy your first view.

Following cairns and blazes, continue to scramble up the successive puddings (there are six), making your way north to the summit. Ocean views to the south, east, and west improve as you climb. Hike up and over ledges, sprinkled generously with low shrubs of juniper and huckleberry. After about 0.9 mile of climbing, finally reach the summit, which is marked indecorously with a subtle USGS marker. From the summit, there are glimpses of Duck Harbor below to the northwest and good views of the western coast of Isle au Haut and offshore islands.

From the summit, descend steeply, watching carefully for cairns and blazes. Dip into the spruce and pine forest and in only 0.3 mile, reach the junction with Western Head Road. Turn right onto the road and walk in a northerly direction about 0.3 mile back to the ferry dock to complete the loop.

CHAPTER

5

Biking
Acadia National Park

Acadia's extensive carriage road system is one of the great treasures of Acadia National Park. Biking is heavenly on these scenic, well-graded gravel roads. Families can choose level lakeside rides or twisting mountain climbs. Ride over beautiful granite bridges, past magnificent spring waterfalls, or through gorgeous forests of autumn foliage. Acadia's carriage roads offer a rich variety of cycling experiences.

The roads visit the park's prettiest ponds and provide splendid picnicking opportunities (trips 23, Witch Hole Pond Loop, 24, Eagle Lake Loop, and 25, Eagle Lake and Bubble Pond). Others hug the sides of mountains and take cyclists to great heights for awesome views of the park (trip 28, Around the Mountain Loop). There are short and easy jaunts (trips 23, 25, and 26, Hadlock Brook Loop), more challenging loops (trip 24, 27, Amphitheater Loop, and 29, Swans Island), and truly strenuous rides (trip 28). For an unusual ride, take the ferry to Swans Island to enjoy quiet island roads (trip 29).

Before setting out on any bike trip, be sure to pack ample liquids, snacks, and helmets for all riders and passengers. At the start of each trip, pick up a park service carriage road map at a roadside dispenser. These maps give cyclists a good overview of the carriage road system, set forth the park's "Rules of the Road," and highlight carriage roads closed to cycling. While riding, use the numbered posts as directional guides (as referred to in the trip descriptions), and do not rely solely on the post's written signage, for the descriptive signs can be misleading. When in doubt, always consult the map and trail description. For more information on the history of these marvelous roads, see chapter 1.

23

Witch Hole Pond Loop

TYPE: Carriage road
DIFFICULTY: Easy
DISTANCE: 3.4 miles round trip; 0.8-mile side trip to
    Paradise Hill; 0.4-mile optional side trip to Break-
    neck Ponds
USAGE: High
STARTING ELEVATION: 200 feet
HIGH POINT: 260 feet
SEASON: Year-round

This perfect family route offers gentle terrain, scenic vistas, ponds, beaver lodges, and delicious late summer blueberries. For the easiest ride, start at the carriage road gate at Duck Brook, a few minutes from Bar Harbor. Those riding from Bar Harbor must climb a fairly long and steep hill to reach the carriage road (see the driving directions below). The route described here begins at the carriage road gate at Duck Brook.

More ambitious cyclists may combine this route with trip 24, Eagle Lake Loop, or trip 25, Eagle Lake and Bubble Pond, for a lovely round trip of about 11.2 miles or 10.6 miles, respectively. This trip's route also makes a fine hike, especially in the fall, when the road is less crowded and the foliage spectacular.

From Bar Harbor, drive west on West Street and cross Route 3 to reach the West Street Extension. Go 0.65 mile up West Street Extension (entering the park after 0.5 mile) to Duck Brook Road. Bear right on Duck Brook Road, pass under the Park Loop Road, and continue 0.75 mile to the top of the hill to a sign indicating

Beaver lodge at Witch Hole Pond

parking for the carriage road. Park the car and ride across the impressive, triple-arched Duck Brook Bridge to Carriage Post 5.

Take a right at Post 5 and coast carefully as the carriage road hugs the edge of the Duck Brook ravine. Be sure to control your speed on the fine gravel. The road swings to the left, passes through a large wet meadow, then approaches a lily pad–covered pond on the right and the northern tip of large Witch Hole Pond on the left.

A fine, abandoned beaver lodge can be seen at the northeast tip of Witch Hole pond, accessible by a trail leading south along the eastern edge of the pond. Dismount and hike in just a few hundred feet for a better view. Along the edge there are classic examples of beaver cuttings: tree stumps that look like they were cut by a giant pencil sharpener. A single quick and efficient beaver can fell a 5-inch-diameter tree in only 3 minutes! Berry pickers can find a fine crop of highbush blueberries growing atop a rock outcropping further south along the pond's eastern shore.

When you return to the carriage road, rise steeply and gain good views of the wetlands to the southeast. Arrive at Post 3 and turn left. Descend 0.2 mile to Post 2, riding along the northern edge of Witch Hole Pond. (For a challenging 0.8-mile addition to this ride, take a right at Post 2 and climb very steeply around the Paradise Hill Loop, taking a right at Post 1. Beyond Post 1, you will be rewarded with truly superb views of Frenchman Bay. Then coast down to Post 3, turn right, and glide back to Post 2.)

At Post 2, all riders should turn left. Look carefully along the edge of Witch Hole Pond for another beaver lodge very close to the carriage road. Anglers have good access here (the pond is stocked with brook trout), as well as those looking for fine picnic spots.

Next travel south on the carriage road, leaving behind Witch Hole Pond. Roll along marshlands, keeping your eye out for ducks and great blue heron. About 0.9 mile from Post 2, arrive at tiny Halfmoon Pond on the right.

Continue on to Post 4. If you are up for a little more riding, a 0.4-mile recommended side trip brings you quickly to two more lovely ponds and more beaver lodges. (From Post 4, turn right and ride just 0.2 mile west to reach Breakneck Ponds. Park your bike and stroll the path that runs along the pond's eastern edge— there are excellent picnic spots along the shore—or cross between the two ponds and stroll down the western shore of the southernmost pond to visit two beaver lodges. These ponds are good places to spy eagles and ring-neck ducks. When you are through exploring,

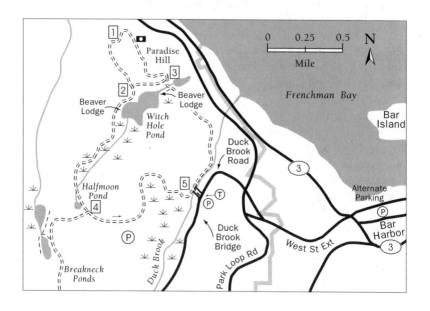

return the way you came to Post 4, and turn right.) If you do not wish to make this side trip, at Post 4 turn left. The carriage road stays fairly level for 1 mile through drier environs back to Duck Brook Bridge. Cross the bridge to the parking area.

To combine this ride with trip 24, Eagle Lake Loop, or trip 25, Eagle Lake and Bubble Pond, from Post 4 take the side trip to Breakneck Ponds and instead of returning to Post 4, ride south from the Breakneck Ponds about 0.9 mile to the Eagle Lake parking area, where these two trips begin.

24

Eagle Lake Loop

TYPE: Carriage road
DIFFICULTY: Moderate
DISTANCE: 6-mile loop; 0.2-mile (one way) optional hike
USAGE: Very high
STARTING ELEVATION: 275 feet
HIGH POINT: 425 feet (588 feet for optional hike)
SEASON: Spring, summer, fall

The Eagle Lake Loop is a challenging family ride. Riders are rewarded with beautiful lake vistas and the opportunity to climb steep Connors Nubble for truly extraordinary views of Mount Desert Island. For anglers, Eagle Lake is stocked with salmon, brook trout, and togue. The only drawback is the midsummer crowd that flocks to this fine ride. Due to heavy bicycle traffic, hiking this route is not recommended except in the off season.

From the intersection of Routes 3 and 233 in Bar Harbor, drive 2.3 miles west on Route 233 to the Eagle Lake parking area, located on the north side of Route 233. Approaching from the west, from the intersection of Routes 233 and 198 at the northeast tip of Somes Sound, the Eagle Lake parking area is 3.5 miles east on Route 233. Park in the Eagle Lake parking area, then follow the gravel path at the parking lot's west side. At the path's intersection with the carriage road, turn left to ride under the stone bridge to Post 6, where the ride begins. (Cyclists combining this trip with trip 23, Witch Hole Pond, continue on from trip 23 to Post 6 by proceeding south 1 mile from Breakneck Ponds to ride under the stone bridge.)

At Post 6, turn left and ride east along the north shore of Eagle Lake. Trees frame the views, and the many oaks, maples, and aspen make this a marvelous fall ride. Arrive quickly at the boat ramp serving Eagle Lake. Large rocks along the shore make wonderful picnic spots with unparalleled views of the Bubbles. (You may want to return to this spot and picnic after you complete the loop.) Remember, however, that swimming in Eagle Lake is strictly prohibited.

Continue riding east on the carriage road as it curves south to follow Eagle Lake's eastern shore. The road rises gently, but the grade is easily handled by most youngsters. Lose the gorgeous views and continue due south about 2 miles from Post 6 to reach Post 7 at the southeastern corner of the lake. At this junction, turn right. (Those who want a shorter, easier course can turn left and follow the directions for trip 25, Eagle Lake and Bubble Pond.)

From Post 7, cyclists climb steeply for almost 1.8 miles, gaining about 150 feet in elevation. After approximately 1.4 miles from Post 7, look to the right for a cedar post marking the trailhead for Connors Nubble. This dramatic 0.2-mile hike is well worth the effort and gives tired cyclists a respite from the grueling uphill ride.

To make this side trip, leave your bike at the post and follow cairns and blazes up the steep, rustic trail. Both arms and legs are needed to scramble up the granite ledges. Youngsters will need help over the tough parts. Reach the quiet summit at 588 feet and reap high rewards. Trees, granite, and gorgeous blue water are spread out in a patchwork of unimaginable beauty. Directly below is Eagle Lake (the largest lake wholly within Acadia National Park), northeast is Frenchman Bay dotted with islands, east is the hulk of Cadillac Mountain, and North and South Bubbles rise to the south (even Bubble Rock is visible!). The bare granite of the Nubble provides a stupendous spot for a picnic. While resting, look skyward for the regal birds that gave this lake its name. When you have drunk your fill of views, carefully retrace your scramble (getting down is a bit tougher), and reclaim your bikes.

Resume your ride and immediately finish the last remaining bit of uphill climb. Then coast down to Post 8. Turn right at Post

8 and proceed north through trees, eventually reaching the western shore of Eagle Lake. Those who do not want to end their ride too quickly can stop and explore a hiking trail along the lake's southwest shore, which provides access to many beautiful and secluded picnic spots among large rocks and pines at the lakeshore.

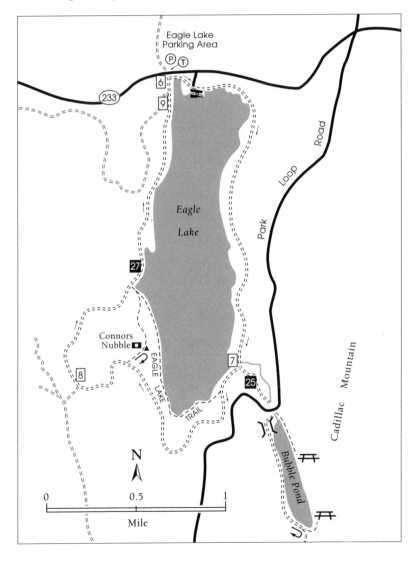

(Find the start of the hiking trail where the carriage road almost meets the lakeshore. Park your bikes and walk south.) Those who don't wish to hike, continue on the carriage road and enjoy a long and gentle stretch for the last rolling mile or so to Post 9, 1.9 miles from Post 8.

At Post 9, continue straight ahead to Post 6. (To revisit the choice picnic area near the ride's beginning, at Post 6 turn right. When you are done with your picnic, retrace your route to Post 6.) To return to the parking area, at Post 6 continue straight, ride under the bridge, then turn right onto the path leading to the parking lot. If the tremendous scenery of Eagle Lake inspires a return visit, try paddling its clear, deep waters (trip 30).

25

Eagle Lake and Bubble Pond

TYPE: Carriage road
DIFFICULTY: Easy
DISTANCE: 2.7 miles one way
USAGE: High
STARTING ELEVATION: 275 feet
HIGH POINT: 325 feet
SEASON: Spring, summer, fall

This short trip is perfect for families seeking a gentle, easy ride. The route hugs the shore of two scenic lakes and provides lots of opportunity for picnicking and exploring. Remember that swimming is prohibited at both Eagle Lake and Bubble Pond, for they are drinking water reservoirs.

Follow the driving directions to the Eagle Lake parking area described in trip 24, Eagle Lake Loop. Follow that trip's riding directions to Post 7, about 2 miles from the parking area.

At Post 7, bear left and ride 0.3 mile to the intersection with the Park Loop Road. Carefully cross the road and arrive at the north end of Bubble Pond. Pretty Bubble Pond lies between the steep eastern slope of Cadillac Mountain and the western slope of

Best friends enjoy Eagle Lake. (Dogs must be leashed!)

Pemetic Mountain. The narrow pond was carved out by the glaciers that formed these impressive mountains. Rimmed with beautiful white cedar, Bubble Pond makes a wonderful destination for young families.

Explorers can leave their bikes and try the informal trail that runs down the eastern shore of the pond. Although the trail disappears after about 0.4 mile, it passes some prime picnicking areas where afternoon sun pleasantly warms the large rocks that line the pond's edge. Bubble Pond is stocked with brook trout, so anglers can try their luck from the scenic shore.

To continue the carriage road ride bear right and cross the bridge at the northern tip of Bubble Pond. The carriage road continues south along the pond's western shore for a very level and scenic 0.7 mile. At the south end of the pond, an informal trail leads to a pebbly beach and some more good picnicking rocks on the pond's far side. After exploring, turn around and retrace the route back to Post 7.

For the easiest ride back (recommended for the youngest riders), bear right at Post 7 and retrace your route back to the Eagle Lake parking area. Those with a sudden burst of energy and enthusiasm can combine this ride with the challenging trip 24, Eagle Lake Loop, by bearing left at Post 7.

26

Hadlock Brook Loop

TYPE: Carriage road
DIFFICULTY: Easy
DISTANCE: 3.9-mile loop
USAGE: High
STARTING ELEVATION: 230 feet
HIGH POINT: 510 feet
SEASON: Spring, summer, fall

This short, immensely enjoyable family ride offers great views, challenging hills, beautiful bridges, and impressive waterfalls. Try it in autumn for terrific fall color.

Drive to the Parkman Mountain parking area. From the intersection of Routes 3 and 233 in Bar Harbor, drive west on Route 233 5.8 miles to its intersection with Routes 198 and 3/198. Turn left onto Route 3/198 and drive south 2.5 miles to the Parkman Mountain parking area on the left (east) side of the road. Approaching from Northeast Harbor, find the parking area by driving north on Route 3/198 1.8 miles from the intersection of Routes

3 and 3/198. Be forewarned that the PARKMAN sign marking the lot is exceedingly small and placed almost opposite the lot.

The carriage road begins at the end of the parking lot. Turn right to reach Post 13. At Post 13, bear left and commence a steep uphill climb. Immediately gain stunning views for your efforts and, in just 0.3 mile, reach Post 12. Bear right at Post 12 and enjoy a more level road.

Ride an easy 0.4 mile to two exquisite bridges almost side by side. Arrive first at the Hemlock Bridge, the first bridge built by J. D. Rockefeller, Jr. It has the longest span of any bridge in Acadia, with a wonderful flourish at either end. Towering hemlocks frame the waterfall behind it.

Ride just 0.1 mile further to cross the beautiful Waterfall Bridge. This bridge provides a perfect platform from which to view

Exploring the Hadlock Brook Bridge

the tallest waterfall in Acadia. Hadlock Brook cascades 40 feet down the handsome granite face of Penobscot Mountain. This is also an excellent place to dismount and explore. Those who want

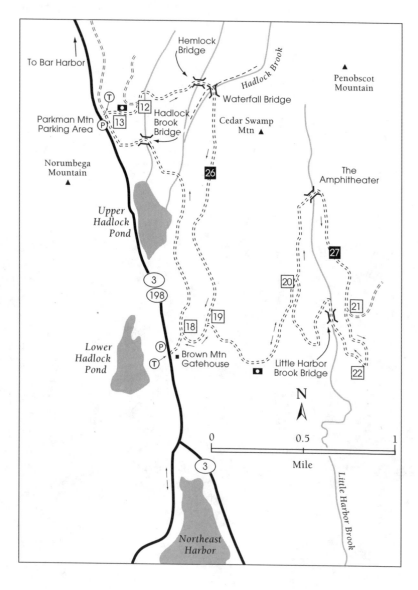

a close-up view of the waterfall can use the Hadlock Brook Trail on the near (north) side of the bridge. The trail runs under the bridge and along Hadlock Brook. Watch for steep drop-offs and slippery rocks beneath the bridge.

After the Waterfall Bridge, enjoy a long downhill stretch through beautiful and varied deciduous woods on the western slope of Cedar Swamp Mountain. To the right are good views over Upper Hadlock Pond. Bear right at Post 19, then continue to coast 0.2 mile down to Post 18.

At Post 18, again bear right and begin a pleasant and level 1-mile stretch. Travel through mixed forest along the shore of Upper Hadlock Pond. Pass over one last lovely carriage bridge, the Hadlock Brook Bridge. The bridge and scenic brook provide a beautiful place for a final rest stop. After the Hadlock Brook Bridge, the road dips then climbs steeply back to Post 13, about 0.7 mile from the bridge. At Post 13, turn left to return to the parking area.

Ambitious cyclists may want to combine the Hadlock Brook Loop with trip 27, Amphitheater Loop, for a very challenging and scenic 8.5-mile loop. To ride the longer course, bear *left* at Post 19, then follow the directions in trip 27, starting at paragraph four.

27

Amphitheater Loop

TYPE: Carriage road
DIFFICULTY: Moderate
DISTANCE: 5.2-mile loop
USAGE: High
STARTING ELEVATION: 200 feet
HIGH POINT: 400 feet
SEASON: Spring, summer, fall

Bicyclists on this moderately challenging ride leave behind crowds and traffic noise to gain scenic vistas and visit two handsome carriage bridges. From expansive views to intimate woodlands,

Enjoying a trailer bike on the Amphitheater Loop

deciduous slopes to pine forest, this loop offers scenic diversity unusual for so short a ride. Yet, like most carriage road routes, this
loop contains some steep sections. After the ride, families can relax in the opulent surroundings of adjacent Northeast Harbor and
can even cycle to the nearby Asticou Terraces and Thuya Garden,
both less than 1 mile from the parking area (see trip 12).

From the intersection of Routes 3 and 233 in Bar Harbor, drive
5.8 miles west on Route 233 to the junction with Routes 198 and
3/198. Turn left and drive south on Route 3/198 3.7 miles to the
parking lot on the left (east) side of the highway, adjacent to the
Brown Mountain Gatehouse. Approaching from Northeast Harbor,
find the parking lot 0.6 mile north of the intersection of Routes 3
and 3/198.

From the parking area, ride onto the carriage road, then immediately turn left and climb a short hill to Post 18. Turn right at Post 18 and ride 0.2 mile to Post 19 and again bear right.

From Post 19, rise on a beautiful stretch of road providing tremendous views of boats sailing in the Western Way and of the picturesque Cranberry Islands. An impressive set of coping stones, affectionately known as "Rockefeller's teeth," creates the road's handsome border. During construction of the granite-faced carriage bridges (financed by J. D. Rockefeller, Jr.), 70 percent of the stones cut did not break along the intended lines and were thus used as coping stones or crushed to cover the roads' surface. After the ascent on this road, it is a welcome coast to Post 20, 0.9 mile from Post 19.

At Post 20, bear left. Rise a bit and after 0.5 mile arrive at impressive Amphitheater Bridge. Those interested in exploring the bridge and underlying Little Harbor Brook may dismount and follow a trail down to the brook under the bridge. In this natural amphitheater, the sounds of wind, rushing water, and bird calls are crystal clear. The fall foliage is superb here also.

After exploring, return to the road and coast down 0.7 mile to Post 21. Keep your family in control, for loose gravel creates hazards on the gently curving road. At Post 21, keep right, continuing downhill 0.4 mile to Post 22. At Post 22, again turn right.

After Post 22, the nature of the road changes as it levels and follows pretty Little Harbor Brook. Find a precious little carriage bridge where the road crosses the brook about 0.5 mile from Post 22. Little Harbor Brook Bridge is an excellent place for a rest stop, a picnic, or an exploring expedition. The small brook babbles soothingly through pretty woods, marked by tall white pines and a soft groundcover of grass and feathery ferns. Young riders may need refreshment to gain strength for the steep stretch of road ahead.

From the bridge, the road rises steeply for more than 0.5 mile. Finally reach Post 20 about 0.7 mile from the bridge, turn left, and climb briefly to the trip's first overlook. Then rejoice that the hard work is over and ride down to Post 19, turn left and continue 0.2 mile to Post 18, and turn left again. The parking area is just ahead.

The Amphitheater Loop can be combined with trip 26, Hadlock Brook Loop, to create a very challenging 8.5-mile loop. See trip 26 for the suggested route.

28

Around the Mountain Loop

TYPE: Carriage road
DIFFICULTY: Strenuous
DISTANCE: 11.1-mile loop
USAGE: High
STARTING ELEVATION: 280 feet
HIGH POINT: 960 feet
SEASON: Spring, summer, fall

This very challenging ride offers spectacular views as it loops around the steep slopes of five mountains: Penobscot, Sargent, Parkman, Bald Peak, and Cedar Swamp. To gain this route's sensational vistas, riders must climb several long, steep hills, one lasting over 2 miles. On the way, cyclists cross seven grand carriage bridges, affectionately named "The Seven Sisters." Ride in spring or early summer to witness fabulous waterfalls cascading down granite streambeds and mountain walls. The ride begins and ends at the Jordan Pond House, where rewards include fine lunches, tea and popovers, and homemade ice cream. This ride is particularly heavenly on a cool fall day, when the foliage is dazzling and the road uncrowded. If your family has time for only one ride and can handle the tough climbs, this route is highly recommended.

Drive to the Jordan Pond parking area, located 0.1 mile north of the Jordan Pond House on the Park Loop Road. From Bar Harbor, at the intersection of Routes 3 and 233, drive west on Route 233 1.1 miles to the intersection with the Park Loop Road (at Acadia's Cadillac Mountain entrance). Turn left onto the Park Loop Road and proceed south approximately 5.1 miles to the Jordan Pond parking area.

Begin your ride from the parking area and ride 0.15 mile south on the Park Loop Road, to the impressive carriage road gatehouse just south of the Jordan Pond House. Turn right on the carriage road and proceed to Post 16. Turn right and coast carefully down to Post 15, then continue straight. Cross a small bridge at the south end of Jordan Pond and climb to Post 14 (see map on p. 86).

Dwarfed by one of the "Seven Sisters"

From Post 14, the directions are very easy to remember. Stay *left* at every junction until the loop is completed and you return to Post 14.

From Post 14, commence a long climb up the eastern slope of Penobscot Mountain. Riders are rewarded with good views of Jordan Pond as they ride along a tremendous rock slide of lichen-mottled pink granite. In fall numerous birch dress the scene in bright yellow.

Beyond the rock slide and north of Jordan Pond, reach the double-arched Deer Brook Bridge, the first of the magnificent "Seven Sisters." Continue north and look down the steep slope to the right where beaver lodges dot the stream valley. At Post 10, 2.1 miles from Post 14, stay left and begin the longest and steepest climb, up the north slope of Sargent Mountain.

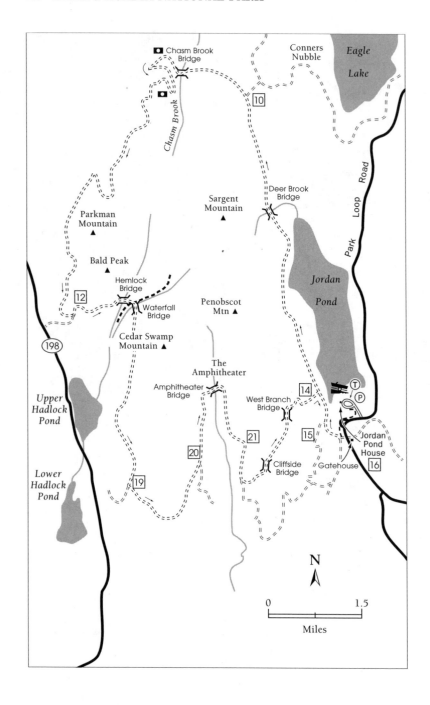

In a few minutes, reach the Chasm Brook Bridge and take a moment to appreciate its wonderful waterfall and dark, grottolike setting. Then ride up steep switchbacks. Hard work is rewarded by excellent views to the northeast of Eagle Lake, with the bare knob of Connors Nubble crowning its south end, and Frenchman Bay in the distance. Continue to rise to almost 800 feet on the northwest slope of Sargent Mountain to truly marvelous views of Somes Sound and sights west.

Finally riders can catch their breath as they descend on the western side of Sargent Mountain. A fairly level stretch follows along the western flanks of Parkman Mountain and Bald Peak. At Post 12, 3.6 miles from Post 10, stay left and resume the climb to reach the unusual gothic arches of Hemlock Bridge. Constructed in 1924, this was the first carriage road bridge built in the park. Exceedingly tall hemlock trees flank the bridge and frame a pretty waterfall. The original plans for the bridge would have necessitated removing the stately trees, so the bridge design was changed to accommodate them. Fifteen men worked year-round for one year using granite cut from local quarries to build the bridge, at a cost of $58,000, paid for (as were all the bridges) by J. D. Rockfeller, Jr. This amount in 1924 seemed excessive even to Rockefeller, so to reduce the cost of subsequent bridges, he ordered their spans shortened and authorized construction only in the summer months.

Immediately after the Hemlock Bridge, cross the Waterfall Bridge over Hadlock Brook. Pause to appreciate Hadlock Brook's beautiful waterfall, the tallest in Acadia. The Hadlock Brook Trail intersects the carriage road at the north end of the bridge. Stroll down the trail for a few hundred yards for an excellent view of the bridge, stream, and magnificent waterfall.

From the bridge, remount and coast down 1.2 miles to Post 19, then stay left and enjoy relatively level riding. Stay left again at Post 20 and climb 0.5 mile to yet another beautiful rough-cut granite bridge, the Amphitheater Bridge. This natural, tree-filled amphitheater is a wonderful spot to enjoy the fall colors. From the bridge, continue on 0.7 mile to Post 21 and stay left. From Post 21, riders cross two more granite bridges, Cliffside Bridge and West Branch Bridge, in the short mile back to Post 14.

At Post 14, take a right to retrace your route past Post 15 to Post 16 and along the Park Loop Road to the parking area. If you are planning to stop at the Jordan Pond House, look for a wood chip path to the left after Post 16, before you arrive at the Park Loop Road. Turn left down this path to reach the Jordan Pond House.

29

Swans Island

TYPE: Paved and unpaved auto roads
DIFFICULTY: Strenuous
DISTANCE: 12.2 miles round trip
USAGE: Low
STARTING ELEVATION: Sea level
HIGH POINT: 150 feet
SEASON: Spring, summer, fall

For a downeast island experience, take the ferry to quiet Swans Island, where cyclists find uncrowded roads, a historic lighthouse, and a lovely, unspoiled, fine-sand beach. Look for seals, seabirds, and porpoises on the scenic 45-minute ferry from Bass Harbor. Then soak up the laid-back island life, as well as the island's fascinating history as a Native American summer encampment, ship building mecca, quarry, and fishery.

The Swans Island Ferry departs from Bass Harbor at the southwest tip of Mount Desert Island. To reach the ferry terminal from Bar Harbor, begin at the intersection of Routes 3 and 233, and drive west on Route 233 5.8 miles to its intersection with Routes 198 and 3/198. Bear right for Route 198 and drive 1.4 miles to Route 198's intersection with Routes 102/198 and 102. Turn left onto Route 102 and drive south about 7.1 miles (stay left when Route 102 splits just south of Somesville) through Southwest Harbor to the junction of Routes 102 and 102A. Turn right onto Route 102 and drive about 1.7 miles to another junction of Routes 102 and 102A. Bear left on 102A and drive 1.3 miles, following numerous signs for the Swans Island Ferry and Bass Harbor. Park

Hockamock Head Lighthouse

in the lot across the street from the ferry building ($3 fee). Purchase ferry tickets at the small terminal building.

Call for a Swans Island ferry schedule (207-244-3254). Round-trip fares are approximately $9 per adult and $5 per child. Bring warm clothing, bicycles, and a picnic lunch. There are a few restaurants and stores on the island, but cyclists may find it more convenient to carry their own provisions. Camping and open fires are prohibited.

The route described here takes cyclists first to the Hockamock Head Lighthouse and then to Fine Sand Beach for a total round-trip distance of 12.2 miles. A side trip to an old quarry (now a fresh-water swimming hole) adds about 4.4 miles round trip. To reverse the direction of this trip's route, simply consult the map of the island provided here.

Upon disembarking the ferry, stop at the terminal to pick up a detailed map of the island and to consult the posted notices for special island events such as a "Downeast" festival or crafts fair. Then leave the terminal and turn right onto the road and ride up a short hill. On the left is the Island Bake Shoppe, which serves breakfast and lunch on outdoor tables overlooking the harbor. Ride up and over the hill 0.5 mile to a stop sign and turn right. Just after this intersection, note the wooden building on the right, the island's historical museum. The one-room museum exhibits photographs and artifacts of the island's rich and colorful past. (Museum hours, Tuesday through Sunday, are 11:00 A.M. to 3:00 P.M.) About 0.3 mile past the museum, the road forks again; stay left on the main road.

Ride the gently rolling road past small, well-tended homes. Pass a quiet, wooded cove on the right and arrive at another fork known as "The Crossroads," about 2 miles from the first fork. Bear right. After another 0.3 mile, pass the Oddfellows Hall (a tall white clapboard building on the right) and stay left at the next intersection. Cycle through the tiny "village" of Swans Island and pass an attractive little pond with ducks and lily pads. Next climb a hill affording excellent views to the left of Burnt Coat Harbor. Pass the Boathouse Restaurant on the left (consider an ice cream cone on the ride back). At about 0.75 mile from the last fork, the road narrows and climbs steeply into woods. Reach the hill's crest, then coast down to a grassy knoll where lonely Hockamock Head

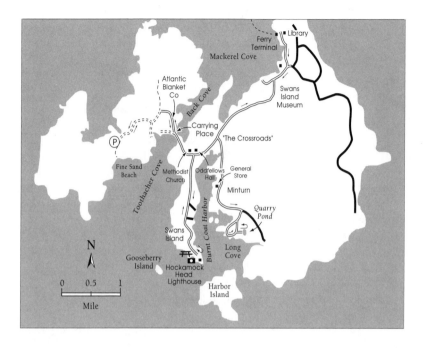

Atlantic Blanket Co

Back Cove

Library
Ferry Terminal
Mackerel Cove

Swans Island Museum

Carrying Place

"The Crossroads"

P

Fine Sand Beach

Toothacher Cove

Methodist Church

Oddfellows Hall

General Store

Minturn

Quarry Pond

Burnt Coat Harbor

Swans Island

Long Cove

N

Gooseberry Island

Hockamock Head Lighthouse

Harbor Island

0   0.5   1

Mile

Lighthouse sits at the entrance to Burnt Coat Harbor, a well-protected cove where lobstering and fishing remain vital to this day. Built in the 1800s, Hockamock Head Lighthouse was continuously staffed until its automation in 1974. All around the lighthouse are lovely places to picnic and take in views of the harbor and offshore islands. The lighthouse's unusual name is of Native American origin.

Next, retrace your route by cycling back to the last main fork in the road that was just past the Oddfellows Hall (a Methodist church is just to the left). To reach Fine Sand Beach, turn left. In 0.5 mile, arrive at a narrow strip of land between two coves, called the "Carrying Place." At this spot, the Native Americans who summered on this island prior to the late 1700s carried their canoes from Toothacher Cove on the south to Back Cove on the north. At low tide, Toothacher Cove sports a pleasant stony beach, while Back Cove hosts extensive muddy clam flats. Each is bordered by fragrant, verdant rugosa roses and prickly raspberry bushes. Stop a moment to beachcomb, or continue on to Fine Sand Beach.

The paved road climbs from the Carrying Place. Just beyond, on the right side of the road, is another interesting stop. Riders can visit the award-winning Atlantic Blanket Company and watch the hand weaving of blankets from local wool. After you pass the blanket company, the road rises steeply. Watch for a wide, unpaved road on the left at the top of the hill, about 0.4 mile from the Carrying Place (it is the second unpaved road on the left). Turn left onto this rough dirt road and ride carefully; keep right at the first fork and continue 0.7 mile to the parking area at the bottom of a hill. Dismount and take the path at the left (south) side of the parking area and hike 0.5 mile through spruce-fir woods to Fine Sand Beach.

The beach is well worth the effort. Its white, sugary sand and shallow water make it a perfect family beach. At low tide the beach is spacious and provides fruitful beach-combing for shells and sand dollars. On either side of the beach, barnacle-covered rocks provide tide pools with an abundance of whelks and periwinkles. Use binoculars to scan the offshore ledges for harbor seals. The beach is isolated and unspoiled.

To return to the ferry dock, or to explore more of the island, retrace the route back past the Carrying Place to the fork in the road near the Methodist Church. Bear left and ride once more past Oddfellows Hall to "The Crossroads." Those heading back to the ferry should bear left at The Crossroads. Riders interested in visiting the Quarry Pond, bear right.

Quarry-bent riders cycle up and down hills for 1.5 miles, through the "village" of Minturn (there is a general store on the right) to arrive at a fork. Bear right and ride 0.7 mile, staying right as the road becomes one way and loops around near the water at Long Cove. On the back side of the loop, just when the road turns north away from the water, look for a road on the right leading uphill. As you look uphill, the semicircular walls of the old granite quarry will be visible. Ride up the short hill and arrive at Quarry Pond. A roped-off area provides freshwater swimming with a beautiful view of the harbor. To return to the ferry dock, continue north on the one-way road until you reach the main route. Turn left and retrace the route back to The Crossroads.

Ferry-bound riders at The Crossroads must ride north about 1.8 miles to the stop sign, then turn left to reach the ferry dock after 0.5 mile. Cold drinks are available at the terminal, and, if there is time to spare, the tiny Swans Island Library located behind the terminal is worth a visit. Alternatively, the Island Bake Shoppe just up the road provides a beautiful perch from which to gaze at the ocean and wait for your boat to come in.

CHAPTER

6

Paddling
Acadia National Park

The beautiful lakes and ponds of Mount Desert Island were created by glacial carving. About 18,000 years ago, a mile-high sheet of ice (four times the present height of Cadillac Mountain!) covered the island. As the ice slowly slid from north to south, the great weight of the ice changed the landscape. The huge glacier swept away everything in its path, rounded the mountains, and "polished" the granite summits to a smooth finish. As the glaciers moved, they also scooped out U-shaped valleys between the mountains. Some of the deeper valleys filled with water and became the pristine lakes we know today. Eagle Lake, Echo Lake, and Long Pond were formed in this manner.

Acadia National Park is a great place for scenic and gentle family paddling adventures. In summer, canoeing and kayaking outings can often be combined with swimming and picnicking (trips 33, Echo Lake, and 34, Long (Great) Pond). In any season, bird-watching and fishing add to the adventure. Choose from a scenic paddle on a very small but beautiful pond (trip 32, Little Long Pond), moderate paddles on larger lakes (trips 30, Eagle Lake, 31, Jordan Pond, 33, and 34) and a challenging paddle on a narrow and twisting creek (trip 35, Northeast Creek).

For all boat trips, families should bring plenty of liquids, wear Coast Guard–approved personal flotation devices, and wear sunscreen or protective clothing. Paddlers should also watch closely for approaching storms or high winds. Lastly, on trips 34, 35, and 38, paddlers must abide by swimming restrictions, for Eagle Lake, Jordan Pond, and Long Pond are drinking water reservoirs.

30

Eagle Lake

TYPE: Waterway for canoes and kayaks; hiking trail from shore
DIFFICULTY: Easy to strenuous
DISTANCE: 5.9-mile loop; 0.6 mile (one way) optional hike
USAGE: Moderate
STARTING ELEVATION: 275 feet; optional hike high point, 588 feet
SIZE OF LAKE: 436 acres
RESTRICTIONS: No swimming (drinking water reservoir)
SEASON: Spring, summer, fall

Rimmed by mountains, Eagle Lake's deep, clear waters and pristine, forested shoreline are a joy to explore. Because Eagle Lake, the second-largest lake on Mount Desert Island, lies wholly within Acadia National Park, there are no vacation homes, major highways, or boat piers to mar the lake's wild quality. Eagle Lake also offers a variety of attractions: shoreline ledges for picnics, trails from the shore for hiking, and angling opportunities including salmon, togue, and brook trout. For the best outing at Eagle Lake, choose a calm day and start early, for the wind often sweeps up the lake in the afternoon, raising whitecaps and making paddling extremely difficult. Remember, too, that swimming is prohibited because Eagle Lake is a drinking water reservoir.

Follow the driving directions for trip 24, Eagle Lake Loop. But instead of parking in the Eagle Lake parking area on the north side of the road, for easy boat access turn into the well-marked

Always bring a map when boating!

Eagle Lake boat launch ramp just a few hundred feet east of the parking area on the south side of the road. Unload the boat, then park in the parking area across the road.

Start your paddle at the boat ramp and proceed south along the west (right) shoreline. Because the lake is so large (436 acres) and deep (110 feet) and its wind conditions so unpredictable, it is recommended that families avoid its open waters by paddling along its nearly 6 miles of lakeshore. By doing so, paddlers will plot a safer course and will have the opportunity to stop and picnic on the inviting ledges at the southwest and southeast shores.

Paddling south, boaters are treated to magnificent views that are particularly colorful in the fall. To the left is Cadillac Mountain, the park's highest. North and South Bubbles and Pemetic Mountain form a backdrop at the lake's south end, and to the right directly above the lake is the small granite knob of Connors Nubble. Further southwest is the immense hulk of Sargent Mountain. Look skyward for soaring osprey and eagles. The latter's presence gave this lake its name over 100 years ago.

About 1.25 miles from the boat ramp, paddlers reach a small cove where a stream enters the lake. From here, a shoreline trail runs along the southwest and south shores of the lake. At the cove's innermost point, paddlers can choose to leave their boats and take a short, but exciting, climb up the steep north side of 588-foot Connors Nubble. This bare granite knob affords tremendous views that far exceed the moderate effort required to scale the

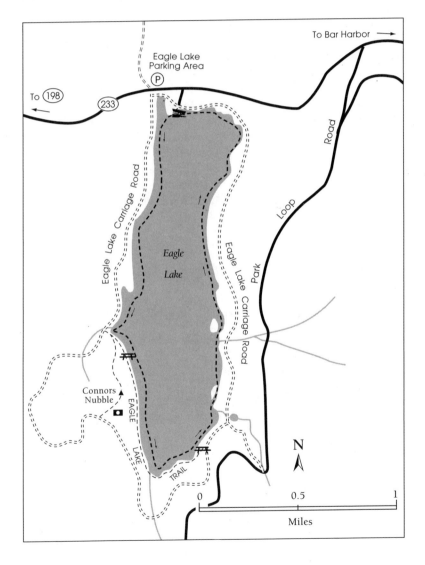

"Nubble." To make the climb, find the start of the lakeshore trail. The trail soon splits; take the right-hand trail. The ascending trail climbs 300 feet quickly to reach the summit in only 0.6 mile. To return from the summit, retrace your steps back to the cove.

Continue to paddle south along the shoreline and look for ledges upon which to rest or picnic. There are some good places near the start of the lakeshore trail just south of the cove, and near the lakeshore trail's end at the southeast end of the lake approximately 2.9 miles from the boat launch.

To return to the boat dock, paddlers can continue along Eagle Lake's east shore, traveling north to return to the boat dock, or they can paddle once more up the lake's west shore. Those paddling up the east shore will pass the former terminus of the cog railroad that brought tourists up Cadillac Mountain almost 100 years ago. For 7 years, a steamboat delivered passengers to the railway from the lake's north end. The steamer, *Wauwinnet,* now lies on the bottom of deep Eagle Lake and little trace of the railroad remains. The loop around the lake is approximately 5.9 miles.

31

Jordan Pond

TYPE: Waterway for canoes and kayaks; hiking trail from shore
DIFFICULTY: Moderate
DISTANCE: 3.5-mile loop; side trip: 0.8 mile round trip
USAGE: Moderate
STARTING ELEVATION: 274 feet; side trip high point, 768 feet
SIZE OF POND: 187 acres
RESTRICTIONS: No swimming (drinking water reservoir)
SEASON: Spring, summer, fall

It is no surprise that the lovely view across Jordan Pond to the Bubbles is found on countless postcards of Acadia National Park.

The Bubbles from Jordan Pond

Jordan Pond is not to be missed. With a canoe or kayak, paddlers can enjoy this rich scenery in relative solitude. Although tourists flock to Jordan Pond by the literal busload, few venture onto its waters. Paddling Jordan Pond can be a relaxing and beautiful excursion, but boaters must be extremely cautious when high winds threaten. As on other ponds in Acadia, winds often whip down the lake between surrounding mountains, creating danger-ous whitecaps. But if families watch the weather and stay near shore, a wonderful adventure awaits.

From the intersection of Routes 3 and 233 in Bar Harbor, drive west 1.1 miles on Route 233 to the Cadillac Mountain entrance. Turn right off Route 233, then left onto the Park Loop Road. Con-tinue south on the Park Loop Road (do not turn left onto the Park

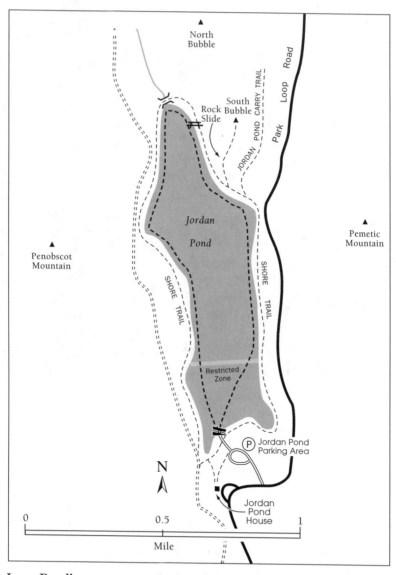

Loop Road's one-way section) and drive south about 5.2 miles to the large parking area for Jordan Pond. The parking area and boat ramp are just 0.2 mile north of the Jordan Pond House. Find the boat launching ramp at the far end of the parking area. From

Route 3 in Seal Harbor, drive north on the Park Loop Road about 2 miles to reach the Jordan Pond parking area.

After launching, paddlers must take a direct route away from the launch area between white buoys through a restricted area that extends approximately 1,000 feet from Jordan Pond's southern shore. The purpose of this restricted zone is to minimize boat traffic near the reservoir's intake pipe. After passing the last buoy, boats are free to roam, but the swimming and wading prohibition remains for the entire pond.

After leaving the restricted zone, paddle north up either side of the pond. Take in the oft-photographed view of the North and South Bubbles (twin rounded peaks) at the pond's north end. Originally, they were known as "The Boobies" for their uncanny resemblance to certain anatomical features. Propriety prevailed, however, as the area was settled, and the name was changed to "The Bubbles."

The northern shore, approximately 1.7 miles from the boat launch, is a good destination; fine picnicking rocks are found on the northeast end of the pond. At the very north end of the pond, there is a nice area for exploring that includes a rocky beach, a wooden bridge, and a large beaver dam and lodge. Beavers are active primarily at night, so boaters are unlikely to see beaver unless they are paddling in the very early morning or at dusk.

To combine paddling and hiking, simply beach your boat anywhere along the shoreline and pick up the well-worn Jordan Pond Shore Trail that runs along the periphery of the entire pond. Another option is to ascend the South Bubble for tremendous views and an opportunity to examine Bubble Rock, a giant glacial erratic perched precariously on the edge of the South Bubble's summit. To climb the South Bubble, paddlers must find the intersection of the Jordan Pond Shore Trail, and the trail heading up the rock slide to the South Bubble. This junction is located approximately two-thirds of the way up the pond on its eastern (right) shore. Hikers must climb 0.4 mile up the rock slide 494 feet to the summit, reversing the direction of the route described in trip 10, South Bubble and Bubble Rock.

On a nice day, families might spend several hours exploring the pond's shoreline. Plot your course, hugging the shore, and leisurely return to the boat launch at the south end of Jordan Pond.

---------------------------------- :**32**: ----------------------------------

Little Long Pond

TYPE: Waterway for canoes and kayaks
DIFFICULTY: Easy
DISTANCE: 1-mile loop
USAGE: Low
STARTING ELEVATION: 8 feet
SIZE OF POND: 38 acres
RESTRICTIONS: None
SEASON: Spring, summer, fall

Little Long Pond is one of the most beautiful places in Acadia National Park. Enjoy its graceful, curving banks, colorful water lilies, shady forest, grassy meadows, and backdrop of mountain summits. These natural elements are so harmonically composed that the effect is more like a magnificent landscape painting than a small inland pond. All who arrive are instantly charmed. And although it takes only an hour or so to explore this little gem by boat, most visitors will want to extend their adventure by hiking the trail described in trip 11, Little Long Pond Loop, or by picnicking in one of its serene meadows or beneath its towering spruce.

To reach Little Long Pond, follow the driving directions for trip 11. Scout the south end of the pond for the easiest put-in. Changing water levels determine the location of the most convenient spot, but good options exist along the south shore or just a few hundred feet up the eastern shore.

Paddle north up the very narrow and shallow southern section of the pond and quickly round a bend to the right. Sight and sounds of the highway mercifully drop away, and the pond widens to reveal glorious Penobscot Mountain and rolling banks of mowed meadows. The private land surrounding the pond is maintained in a parklike manner by the Rockefeller family. Through their generosity, the public is free to enjoy the grounds.

On the right (east) bank, about 0.25 mile from the put-in, is the old Rockefeller boathouse. On its far side is a tiny beach, perfect for wading. Just beyond is a spruce-covered point that makes

Exploring the forest near Little Long Pond

an exquisite picnic spot. Equally inviting on both the right and left banks are dry meadows. For the most privacy, try picnicking in the west bank meadow. A path, more rustic and less traveled than the east shore trails, runs up the west shore of the pond, in and out of shady woods.

Paddle north, past the boathouse, until the pond turns to marsh at the inlet of Jordan Stream. This is an excellent place to look for birds. Great blue heron often feed at the marsh. These impressive blue-gray birds stand 4 feet tall and have wingspans of about 6 feet. Herons can be seen wading knee-deep in the pond, patiently waiting to spear an unsuspecting fish or frog with their long, yellow beaks.

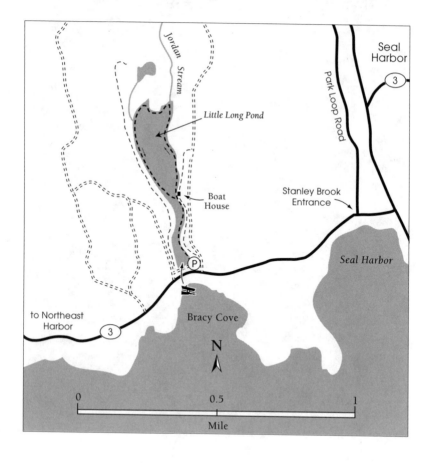

Before turning around, take a look at the beaver lodge in the reeds at the northeast end of the pond. Sharp eyes can spot signs of beaver (stumps and felled trees) along the pond's west shore. When you can paddle no further, about 0.5 mile from the put-in, return to the pond's south end.

33

Echo Lake

TYPE: Waterway for canoes and kayaks
DIFFICULTY: Easy
DISTANCE: 2-mile loop
USAGE: High
STARTING ELEVATION: 84 feet
SIZE OF LAKE: 237 acres
RESTRICTIONS: None
SEASON: Spring, summer, fall

Echo Lake, immensely popular with young families, boasts a convenient boat ramp, easily accessible ledges for swimming, scenic granite cliffs, and a sandy beach equipped with lifeguards and changing facilities. Though its setting is less pristine than other lakes on Mount Desert Island (busy Route 102 runs up its eastern shore), Echo Lake's sandy beach and warm water are sure to please youngsters on a hot summer's day.

From the junction of Routes 3 and 233 in Bar Harbor, drive west on Route 233 5.8 miles to its junction with Routes 198 and 3/198. Bear right on Route 198 and proceed 1.4 miles to the junction of Routes 198/102 and 102. Bear left on Route 102 (to Somesville) and drive south 3.1 miles to the turnout for Ikes Point on the right (west) side of the highway. The boat launch is at the end of the parking area.

For a family-pleasing summer's paddle, from the boat launch head south along the east shore of Echo Lake. After about 0.25 mile, arrive at "the Ledges," a popular, unofficial swimming spot.

Sand castle building on Echo Lake Beach

Flat granite ledges along the shore provide jumping-off points for older youngsters.

After a dip, continue south past an Appalachian Mountain Club summer camp. In another 0.25 mile, arrive at Echo Lake Beach on the south shore. Watch for swimmers, and do not enter the roped-off restricted area. Families who wish to swim, sun, snorkel, or build sand castles could take a break here.

To continue the loop, paddle north along the west side of Echo Lake beneath the sheer granite walls of Beech Cliff. Lucky paddlers may spy the eagles or even the peregrine falcons that occasionally nest on the cliffs. Almost always, intrepid climbers are visible on Beech Cliff's steep ladder trail.

Paddle about 0.6 mile north from Echo Lake Beach until Ikes Point is visible across the lake. To return to the launch, paddle across the lake and back to Ikes Point. A longer loop around Echo Lake is possible, but it is not recommended because the northern shore of the lake is privately owned, and Route 102 runs very close to the lake's east shore.

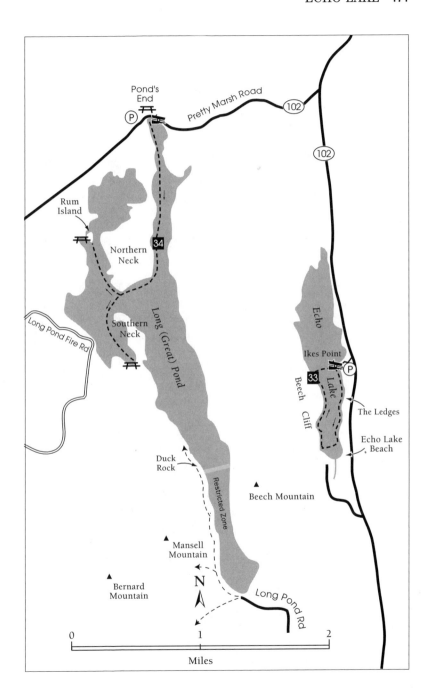

Pond's End

Pretty Marsh Road

102

102

Rum Island

Northern Neck

34

Long (Great) Pond

Southern Neck

Long Pond Fire Rd

Echo Lake

Ikes Point

33

Beech Cliff

The Ledges

Echo Lake Beach

Duck Rock

Restricted Zone

Beech Mountain

Mansell Mountain

Bernard Mountain

N

Long Pond Rd

0   1   2

Miles

34

Long (Great) Pond

TYPE: Waterway for canoes and kayaks
DIFFICULTY: Moderate
DISTANCE: 3.8-mile loop
USAGE: High
STARTING ELEVATION: 59 feet
SIZE OF POND: 897 acres
RESTRICTIONS: No swimming in southern third of
    pond (drinking water reservoir)
SEASON: Spring, summer, fall

Visit Long Pond, Mount Desert Island's largest lake, on a warm summer day for a full day of family fun. Rent canoes pondside, paddle to islands and ledges for superb picnicking, and swim in the pond's clear and temperate water. Long Pond's only drawbacks are its popularity with motorboats and the many private homes dotting its eastern shore. Also, paddling should be attempted only when the wind is calm, for water conditions on Long Pond become treacherous when the northerly winds begin to blow.

From the intersection of Routes 3 and 233 in Bar Harbor, drive west on Route 233 5.8 miles to its intersection with Routes 198 and 3/198. Bear right and take Route 198 0.4 mile to another junction. Turn left (south) on Route 102 and drive 0.8 mile (through Somesville) to a fork where Route 102 splits in two. Take the right-hand fork of Route 102 (also known as Pretty Marsh Road) and proceed 1.4 miles to Long Pond on the left (south) side of the road.

For those renting canoes, canoe rentals are across the street and there is ample parking in the lot behind the rental hut. There is also limited parking at the north end of the pond near the pier and boat launch. This area, called Pond's End, offers protected swimming with a gently graded beach perfect for young swimmers. Other amenities at Pond's End include a grassy area for picnicking, shade trees, and portable toilets.

From the put-in at Pond's End, there are two scenic areas to explore by boat. Both are reached by paddling south down the mile-long western shore, along the Northern Neck. At the end of

Northern Neck, bear right (west) and paddle about 0.4 mile around the head of the neck.

At the end of the neck, boaters have two options. By paddling north about 0.5 mile, paddlers reach tiny Rum Island, part of Acadia National Park, where families can explore, picnic, and swim. Alternatively, paddlers can head about 0.5 mile south to the protected cove west of Southern Neck, where calm water, excellent swimming spots, and picnicking ledges abound. Since most of the western shore of Long Pond, including Southern Neck, is part of Acadia National Park, the scenery becomes more pristine and agreeable. (Visit both of these enticing spots for a round-trip paddle of about 4.8 miles from the launch at Pond's End.)

Canoeing on Long Pond

:35:

Northeast Creek

TYPE: Waterway for canoes and kayaks
DIFFICULTY: Moderate
DISTANCE: 1.5 miles one way
USAGE: Low
STARTING ELEVATION: 10 feet
RESTRICTIONS: None
SEASON: Spring, summer, fall

Try Northeast Creek for one of the finest paddling experiences on Mount Desert Island. This narrow creek winds past deciduous forest and through acres of wide-open heath offering serene vistas of high hills and distant mountains. In late summer, blueberries grow along its banks, and in autumn, deep red cranberries ripen at water's edge. In fall, the colors are glorious. In all seasons, the sense of solitude and quiet on the creek is sublime. Although Northeast Creek runs mostly through private property, paddlers see few signs of civilization. And while on most days the sepia-colored water flows gently, rising winds across the heath can suddenly make paddling extremely difficult and even dangerous. Paddlers must be alert to weather conditions at all times.

Experienced paddlers may want to visit Northeast Creek on a calm, moonlit night. Darkness enhances the creek's serenity and adds an air of mystery and adventure. Marsh and forest inhabitants, such as great blue herons, owls, and whitetail deer, may be seen or heard. In any event, gliding through the dark water under a full moon promises to be a magical experience.

Drive to the put-in at the north end of Mount Desert Island near the Thompson Island visitor center. To reach the put-in from the Trenton Bridge at the head of Mount Desert Island, drive east on Route 3 about 2 miles to the bridge over Northeast Creek. From the junction of Routes 3 and 233 in Bar Harbor, drive west on Route 233 5.8 miles to its junction with Route 198 and 3/198. Bear right on Route 198 and drive 1.4 miles to the junction of Routes 102/198 and 102. Turn right and drive north on Route 102/198

A young kayaker gets ready to roll.

about 2.3 miles, to the tiny "town" of Town Hill and the route's intersection with Knox Road. Bear right on Knox Road and drive about 1.5 miles to its intersection with Route 3. Turn right on Route 3 and drive 0.5 mile to the bridge over Northeast Creek. Find the dirt put-in on the north (far) side of the bridge.

Proceed up the creek from the put-in, traveling southeast down a narrow channel. Maples and aspens adorn the banks, and waterfowl cruise the tea-colored water. Paddlers must watch for large rocks just beneath the surface, especially at the point where the creek takes a sharp turn to the right, about 0.75 mile from the put-in. The rocks in the creek are remnants of an old dam that once flooded the surrounding marsh for cranberry farming.

After the turn, paddlers enter the wide-open heath called Fresh Meadow. After paddling for about 0.5 mile through Fresh

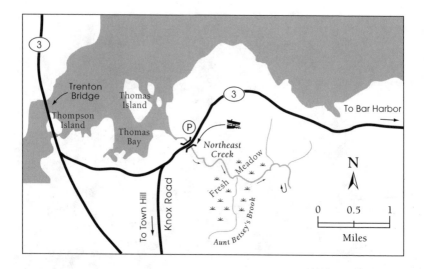

Meadow, you will see Aunt Betsey's Brook entering from the right. Stay on the main channel. After another 0.5 mile, pass between a wooded hill on the right and high, dry ground on the left. The creek then swings south (to the right) and becomes increasingly narrow as it pushes through cattails and marsh grass. Paddlers soon are forced to turn around and retrace their route to the bridge.

Appendix A
Trip Finder

Key to Symbols

Difficulty: VE = very easy; E = easy; M = moderate;
S = strenuous

Mileage: RT = round trip; OW = one way

Usage: L = low; M = moderate; H = high; VH = very high

Handicap access with assistance: (H*)

Points of interest: P = peak; S = swimming;
H = historical interest; W = waterfall; FF = fall
foliage; TP = tide pooling; F = fishing; G = gardens;
Geo = geological formations; C = rock climbing; BW=
wildlife/bird-watching

Hiking Eastern Acadia NP

	Difficulty	Mileage	Usage	Points of Interest
1. Great Head Trail—*hiking trail*	M	1.5 miles RT	H	S, Geo, C, BW
2. Ocean Trail—*hiking trail*	E	2.0 miles OW	VH	S, Geo, TP, BW
3. The Beehive Loop—*hiking trail*	S	1.5 miles RT	H	P, FF, Geo, C
4. Gorham Mountain and the Bowl Loop—*hiking trail*	M	4.5 miles RT	H	P, S, FF, Geo, BW
5. South Ridge of Cadillac Mountain—*hiking trail*	S	3.7 miles OW	M	P, Geo, FF
6. Jesup Trail/Hemlock Road Loop—*hiking trail*	E	1.4 miles RT	M	FF, G, BW
7. Hunters Beach—*hiking trail*	E	0.5 mile OW	L	TP, S

	Difficulty	Mileage	Usage	Points of Interest
8. Penobscot and Sargent Mountains—*hiking trail*	S	2.6 miles OW	H	P, S, FF, Geo, C
9. Pemetic Mountain—*hiking trail*	S	3.2 miles RT	L	P, FF, Geo, C
10. South Bubble and Bubble Rock—*hiking trail*	M-S	2.0 miles RT	H	P, FF, Geo, C
11. Little Long Pond Loop (H*)—*hiking trail*	VE	1.4 miles RT	M	S, H, FF, W
12. Asticou Terraces, Thuya Garden, and Eliot Mountain—*hiking trail*	E–M	0.5–1.1 miles OW	L–H	P, H, G
Hiking Western Acadia NP				
13. Valley Trail and Beech Mountain Loop—*hiking trail*	M	2.9 miles RT	M	P, H, FF, Geo, W
14. Mansell Mountain—*hiking trail*	S	3.3 miles RT	L	P, H, FF, C
15. Bernard Mountain—*hiking trail*	M	1.6 miles OW	L	P, FF
16. Ship Harbor Nature Trail—*self-guided nature trail*	E	1.3 miles RT	H	H, TP, W
17. Wonderland Trail (H*)—*hiking trail*	E	0.7 mile OW	H	TP, W
18. Indian Point Woods and Shore Trail—*hiking trail*	VE	0.7 mile RT	M	W
Hiking Isle au Haut and the Schoodic Peninsula				
19. Little Moose Island—*hiking trail*	E	1.3 miles OW	L	TP, W
20. Anvil Trail—*hiking trail*	M	1.0 mile OW	L	P, Geo, C, W
21. Western Head and Cliff Trails—*hiking trail*	M	4.1 miles RT	L	TP, W

22. Goat Trail and Duck Harbor Mountain Trail—*hiking trail*	S	3.6 miles RT	L	P, BW, Geo, C
Biking Acadia NP				
23. Witch Hole Pond Loop—*carriage rd*	E	3.4 miles RT	H	FF, F (trout), W
24. Eagle Lake Loop—*carriage rd / hiking trail*	M	6.0 miles RT 0.4-mile hike	VH	P, FF, F (salmon, brook trout), C, BW
25. Eagle Lake and Bubble Pond—*carriage rd*	E	2.7 miles OW	H	FF, F (brook trout)
26. Hadlock Brook Loop—*carriage rd*	E	3.9 miles RT	H	W, FF
27. Amphitheater Loop—*carriage rd*	M	5.2 miles RT	H	W, FF
28. Around the Mountain Loop—*carriage rd*	S	11.1 miles RT	H	W, FF
29. Swans Island—*paved / unpaved auto rd*	S	12.2 miles RT	L	S, H, TP, BW
Paddling Acadia NP				
30. Eagle Lake—*canoe or kayak / hiking trail*	E–S	5.9 miles RT 1.2-mile hike	M	FF, F (brook trout), P, C, BW
31. Jordan Pond—*canoe or kayak / hiking trail*	M	3.5 miles RT 0.8-mile hike	M	FF, F (trout, togue, salmon), P
32. Little Long Pond—*canoe or kayak*	E	1 mile RT	L	FF, S, BW
33. Echo Lake—*canoe or kayak*	E	2 miles RT	H	S, BW
34. Long (Great) Pond—*canoe or kayak*	M	3.8 miles RT	H	Sw, FF, F (bass, salmon, smelt), BW
35. Northeast Creek—*canoe or kayak*	M	1.5 miles OW	L	FF, BW

Appendix B
Recommended Reading

Build upon your family's experiences in Acadia National Park through excellent books on nature and regional history. The following list includes books that promote an awareness of, sensitivity to, and enjoyment of the environment. Many are available at the park visitor center.

The Eastern National Park and Monument Association is an excellent resource for top-quality nature books for all ages. This nonprofit organization operates the bookstore at the visitor center and also sells publications through the mail. To receive a list of publications, write the Eastern National Park and Monument Association (Acadia National Park, P.O. Box 177, Bar Harbor, ME 04609-0177) or call (207) 288-4988. Members of the association receive a discount on all purchases.

The following organizations also offer nature books by mail: National Wildlife Federation (1400 16th Street NW, Washington, D.C. 20036; 1-800-432-6564), National Geographic Society, Educational Services (P.O. Box 2118, Washington, D.C. 20013-2118; 1-800-368-2728), and The Sierra Club (730 Polk Street, San Francisco, CA, 94109; 415-923-5500).

FIELD GUIDES FOR CHILDREN
Alden, Peter. *Peterson First Guide to Mammals*. Boston: Houghton Mifflin, 1987.
Arnosky, Jim. *Secrets of a Wildlife Watcher—A Beginner Field Guide*. New York: Beech Tree Books, 1991.
Murie, Olaus J. *Animal Tracks*. Peterson Field Guides. Boston: Houghton Mifflin, 1974.
Peterson, Roger Tory. *Birds—A Simplified Field Guide*. Boston: Houghton Mifflin, 1986.
———. *Wildflowers—A Simplified Field Guide to Common Wildflowers*. Boston: Houghton Mifflin, 1986.
Scheid, Margaret. *Discovering Acadia—A Guide for Young Naturalists*. Bar Harbor, Maine: Acadia Press, 1988.

GENERAL NONFICTION FOR CHILDREN

Arnosky, Jim. *Crinkleroot's Guide to Walking in Wild Places.* New York: Simon & Schuster, 1990.

The Earthworks Group. *Fifty Simple Things Kids Can Do to Save the Earth.* New York: Universal Press Syndicate, 1990.

Foster, Lynne. *Take a Hike! The Sierra Club's Beginner Guide to Hiking and Backpacking.* Boston: Little, Brown, 1991.

Gibbons, Gail. *Surrounded by Sea – Life on a New England Fishing Island.* Boston: Little, Brown, 1991.

PICTURE BOOKS

Donahue, Mike. *The Grandpa Tree.* Boulder, Colo.: Roberts Rinehart, 1988.

Evans, Lisa Gollin. *An Elephant Never Forgets Its Snorkel.* New York: Crown Books, 1992.

McCloskey, Robert. *Blueberries for Sal.* New York: Puffin Books, 1976.

———. *One Morning in Maine.* New York: Puffin Books, 1976.

Pallotta, Jerry. *Going Lobstering.* Watertown, Mass.: Charlesbridge Publishing, 1990.

Roop, Peter, and Connie Roop. *Keep the Lights Burning, Abbie.* Minneapolis, Minn.: Lerner Group, 1985.

Seus, Dr. *The Lorax.* New York: Random House, 1971.

Svedberg, Ulf. *Nicky the Nature Detective.* New York: Farrar, Straus & Giroux, 1988.

PERIODICALS FOR CHILDREN

National Geographic World. National Geographic Society, P.O. Box 2118, Washington, D.C. 20013-2118; 1-800-368-2728. Ages 8–14.

Ranger Rick. National Wildlife Federation, 1400 West 16th Street NW, Washington, D.C. 20036; 1-800-432-6564. Ages 6–12.

Your Big Backyard. National Wildlife Federation, 1400 West 16th Street NW, Washington, D.C. 20036; 1-800-432-6564. Ages 3–5.

Zoobooks. Wildlife Education Ltd., P.O. Box 28870, San Diego, CA 92128. Ages 4–12.

BOOKS FOR PARENTS

Brown, Tom, Jr. *Tom Brown's Guide to Nature and Survival for Children*. New York: Berkley Publishing Group, 1989.

Carson, Rachel. *The Sense of Wonder*. New York: Harper and Row, 1984.

Cornell, Joseph Bharat. *Sharing Nature with Children*. Nevada City, Calif.: Dawn Publications, 1979.

Peterson, Carol, and Margaret Scheid. *Activity Guide to Acadia National Park for Teachers, Youth Leaders and Interested Parents*.

FIRST-AID BOOKS

Gill, Paul G., Jr. *Simon and Schuster's Pocket Guide to Wilderness Medicine*. New York: Fireside Books, 1991.

Lentz, Martha J., Steven D. MacDonald, and Jan D. Carline. *Mountaineering First Aid*. Seattle, Wash.: The Mountaineers, 1985.

NATURAL HISTORY AND REGIONAL GUIDEBOOKS

Abrell, Diana F. *A Pocket Guide to the Carriage Roads of Acadia National Park*. Camden, Maine: Down East Books, 1995.

Brechlin, Earl D. *Hiking on Mount Desert Island*. Camden, Maine: Down East Books, 1996.

———. *Paddling the Waters of Mount Desert Island*. Camden, Maine: Down East Books, 1996.

Eastern National Park and Monument Association. *Acadia National Park — Motorists Guide*. Bar Harbor: Acadia Publishing, 1991.

Elfring, Chris. *Appalachian Mountain Guide to Mount Desert Island and Acadia National Park*. Boston: Appalachian Mountain Club, 1993.

Gillmore, Robert. *Great Walks — Acadia National Park and Mount Desert Island*. Goffstown, N.H.: Great Walks, 1994.

Lewis, Cynthia C., and Thomas J. Lewis. *Best Hikes with Children in Vermont, New Hampshire, and Maine*. Seattle, Wash.: The Mountaineers, 1991.

Minutolo, Audrey. *Biking on Mount Desert Island*. Camden, Maine: Down East Books, 1996.

Newlin, William. *The Down East Guide to the Lakes and Ponds of Mt. Desert.* Camden, Maine: Down East Books, 1989.

St. Germain, Tom. *A Walk in the Park: Acadia's Hiking Guide.* Bar Harbor, Maine: Parkman Publications, 1994.

———. *Acadia's Biking Guide and Carriage Road Handbook.* Bar Harbor, Maine: Parkman Publications, 1995.

Appendix C
Conservation Organizations

The following organizations are working to protect, enhance, and improve the invaluable natural resources in and around Acadia National Park. To play a part in preserving this most beautiful and historic park, contact one or more of the organizations listed below.

National Park Service: Acadia National Park, P.O. Box 177, Bar Harbor, ME 04609; (207) 288-2564

Help maintain Acadia National Park's superlative interpretive program by contributing to donation boxes located at the park visitor center, the Nature Center, and the Islesford Historical Museum on Little Cranberry Island. In view of diminishing federal funds for national parks, public donations play an increasingly important role in maintaining park programs. In 1996, public donations paid the salaries of four rangers and helped to enlarge the visitor center building. Donations at the Islesford Historical Museum supported one student intern and the purchase of new, weathertight doors. Continued public support will ensure that superior public education programs continue and that infrastructure needs are met.

Another way that you can make a valuable contribution to Acadia National Park is to volunteer to help maintain the park's historic trails and carriage roads. Volunteers can spend a few hours helping mark trails, clipping brush, and raking leaves from carriage road ditches. It is a great way to meet new friends and experience the value of community service. For information on how you can volunteer, call the park service.

Friends of Acadia, P.O. Box 725, Bar Harbor, ME 04609; (207) 288-3340; outside Maine, 800-914-4415; e-mail address: eileen @foa.acadia.net

Established as a nonprofit in 1986, Friends of Acadia is a superb service organization whose projects substantially benefit Acadia National Park. The Friends have undertaken more than thirty separate initiatives designed to educate, preserve, protect, and maintain a quality resource for visitors and residents. Their achievements include more than a million-dollar increase in the park's annual budget; raising $8 million for restoration and permanent maintenance of the historic carriage roads; a volunteer trail maintenance program that substantially improved the park's 120 miles of hiking trails; a grant that has helped re-establish peregrine falcons in the park; an environmental education program for area schools; and a Resource Sensitive Tourism program that has helped educate residents, visitors, area businesses, and state government about the need to protect the region's natural resources. With a donation of $35 or more, you can become a member. Members receive the informative quarterly *Journal* and *Acadia Report.*

The Nature Conservancy, Maine Chapter, Fort Andross, 14 Maine Street, Suite 401, Brunswick, ME 04011; (207) 729-5181

The Nature Conservancy is an international conservation organization dedicated to preserving plants, animals, and natural communities that represent the diversity of life by protecting the lands and waters they need to survive. Since 1950, the conservancy has protected over eight million acres in fifty states, Latin America, the Virgin Islands, Canada, and the Caribbean. The Maine chapter, formed in 1956, has protected over 100,000 acres of land, including the very beautiful Indian Point–Blagden Preserve on the western side of Mount Desert Island. You can help to preserve Maine's unique natural heritage by enrolling as a member of The Nature Conservancy.

Adopt a Finback Whale, The Finback Catalogue, College of the Atlantic, 105 Eden Street, Bar Harbor, ME 04609; (207) 288-5644; fax (207) 288-4126

By "adopting" a finback whale, you can help protect the second-largest mammal ever to inhabit the earth. Although listed as an endangered species in the United States, the whales are still hunted in some parts of the world, including the North Atlantic Ocean. Threats to their habitat, such as pollution, ocean dumping, shipping, destructive fishing practices, and coastal development, also endanger the lives of these magnificent creatures. Adopting a finback whale is your investment in the growing understanding of this endangered species. Your contribution is important in the effort to save them for future generations. When you adopt a finback whale, your contribution assists researchers working to understand the life history of this endangered animal. Contributors receive an 8-by-12-inch color photograph and a brief history of your whale, *The Adopt a Finback Whale Book* of photos and information about whales and whale research, a personal Certificate of Adoption, and a semi-annual newsletter.

Index

About the Author

Lisa Gollin Evans received her B.A. from Cornell University, then obtained a J.D. from Boalt Hall School of Law. Between books Evans works in the field of environmental law, most recently for the Massachusetts Department of Coastal Zone Management.

Evans believes that the best way to create tomorrow's environmentalists is to expose children to the wonders, beauty, and excitement of nature. Her books include *An Outdoor Family Guide to Rocky Mountain National Park, An Outdoor Family Guide to Lake Tahoe,* and *An Outdoor Family Guide to Yellowstone and Grand Teton National Parks.* She has also written a nonfiction book for children, *An Elephant Never Forgets Its Snorkel,* which was named an "Outstanding Science Book for Children" in 1992 by the National Association of Science Teachers and the Children's Book Council. Evans lives with her husband and three daughters in Marblehead, Massachusetts.

THE MOUNTAINEERS, founded in 1906, is a nonprofit outdoor activity and conservation club, whose mission is "to explore, study, preserve, and enjoy the natural beauty of the outdoors. . . ." Based in Seattle, Washington, the club is now the third-largest such organization in the United States, with 15,000 members and five branches throughout Washington State.

The Mountaineers sponsors both classes and year-round outdoor activities in the Pacific Northwest, which include hiking, mountain climbing, ski-touring, snowshoeing, bicycling, camping, kayaking and canoeing, nature study, sailing, and adventure travel. The club's conservation division supports environmental causes through educational activities, sponsoring legislation, and presenting informational programs. All club activities are led by skilled, experienced volunteers, who are dedicated to promoting safe and responsible enjoyment and preservation of the outdoors.

If you would like to participate in these organized outdoor activities or the club's programs, consider a membership in The Mountaineers. For information and an application, write or call The Mountaineers, Club Headquarters, 300 Third Avenue West, Seattle, WA 98119; (206) 284-6310.

The Mountaineers Books, an active, nonprofit publishing program of the club, produces guidebooks, instructional texts, historical works, natural history guides, and works on environmental conservation. All books produced by The Mountaineers are aimed at fulfilling the club's mission.

Send or call for our catalog of more than 300 outdoor titles:

The Mountaineers Books
1001 SW Klickitat Way, Suite 201
Seattle, WA 98134
1-800-553-4453 / e-mail: mbooks@mountaineers.org

Other titles you may enjoy from The Mountaineers:

An Outdoor Family Guide to Yellowstone and Grand Teton National Parks, Lisa Gollin Evans
New comprehensive guide to forty-eight outings in these majestic national parks. Includes the best family-friendly hikes, bike tours, and paddling trips.

An Outdoor Family Guide to Lake Tahoe, Lisa Gollin Evans
Fifty-three short hikes and bike rides within driving distance of Lake Tahoe. Complete trail descriptions, plus information on flora, fauna, history, environmental awareness, safety, and more.

Kids in the Wild: A Family Guide to Outdoor Recreation, Cindy Ross & Tom Gladfelter
A family-tested handbook of advice on sharing outdoor adventures with children of all ages and skill levels.

Best Hikes with Children™ in Vermont, New Hampshire, and Maine, Cynthia & Thomas Lewis
Guide to seventy-nine day hikes and overnighters for families. Includes tips on hiking with kids, safety, points of interest, and more.